Trade Phenomena

The Path to Self-Reliance

Embark on a transformative journey into the world of trading with "Trade Phenomena." This comprehensive guide seamlessly blends the time-tested strategies of trading legends with the innovative approaches of cryptocurrency professionals. From historical tactics to modern insights, learn to navigate financial markets with precision, cultivate resilience, and achieve self-reliance. Whether you're a novice or seasoned trader, this book empowers you to take control of your financial destiny. Welcome to a new era of trading wisdom.

TK RANA

DEDICATION

Dedicated to all the aspiring traders and investors who believe in the transformative power of self-reliance. May your journey through the markets be filled with wisdom, resilience, and the joy that comes from navigating the path to financial empowerment. This book is dedicated to empowering you to take charge of your trading destiny and discover the happiness that arises from mastering the art of self-reliance in every market venture.

CONTENTS

ACKNOWLEDGMENTS

In the creation of "Trade Phenomena: The Path to Self-Reliance," I extend my deepest gratitude to the individuals whose contributions and support have played a pivotal role in bringing this project to fruition.

I would like to express my appreciation to the trailblazing traders, both historical and contemporary, whose innovative strategies and wisdom have inspired the content of this book. Their insights form the foundation upon which "Trade Phenomena" stands.

A heartfelt thank you goes to the mentors, educators, and experts whose guidance has shaped my understanding of the financial markets. Your knowledge has been instrumental in crafting a resource that aims to empower and enlighten traders at every level.

I extend my thanks to the dedicated professionals in the financial industry whose commitment to excellence has set a standard worth aspiring to. Your collective impact on the world of trading is acknowledged and celebrated within these pages.

To my readers, whose curiosity and enthusiasm for mastering the art of self-reliant trading have driven the creation of this book, I am grateful for your engagement and trust. May "Trade Phenomena" serve as a valuable companion on your journey to financial independence.

Finally, to my family and friends, whose unwavering support and encouragement have been a source of strength, thank you for being the pillars of my success. Your belief in this endeavor has made it all the more meaningful.

This book stands as a testament to the collaborative spirit that drives progress. It is with sincere gratitude that I acknowledge the collective effort that has brought "Trade Phenomena: The Path to Self-Reliance" to life.

CHAPTER 1

TRADING STRATEGIES

Embark on a journey into the dynamic world of trading strategies in "Trade Phenomena: The Path to Self-Reliance." This foundational chapter lays the groundwork for your exploration into the art and science of successful trading.

Topics Covered:

❖ **Short-term Trading Strategies:**
Dive into the fast-paced realm of short-term trading, exploring tactics designed to capitalize on intraday or short-term market fluctuations. Uncover the strategies employed by seasoned traders to navigate rapid market movements and seize immediate opportunities.

❖ **Medium-term Trading Strategies:**
Navigate the middle ground between short-term and long-term trading as we delve into medium-term strategies. Discover how these approaches aim to capture trends and price movements over a more extended timeframe, balancing agility with a more comprehensive market view.

❖ **Long-term Investment Strategies:**
Explore the patient and strategic world of long-term investment strategies. Understand the principles behind holding assets for extended periods, harnessing the power of compounding, and building wealth over time. Gain insights into identifying assets with enduring value and potential

for sustainable growth.

❖ Common Strategies Across All Time Horizons:

Identify the common threads that weave through short-term, medium-term, and long-term strategies. Uncover overarching principles and techniques that transcend time horizons, providing a holistic perspective on effective trading approaches.

❖ Trading Strategies: Dos and Don'ts for Success:

Learn the essential do's and don'ts that guide successful traders. Understand the critical factors that contribute to effective strategy implementation and discover pitfalls to avoid. Develop a comprehensive understanding of the best practices for navigating the complexities of financial markets.

❖ Benefits of Trading Strategies:

Explore the tangible benefits that well-crafted trading strategies bring to investors. From consistent returns to risk mitigation, understand how strategic approaches enhance the overall trading experience and contribute to long-term success.

❖ Risks of Trading Strategies:

Delve into the potential risks associated with trading strategies. Recognize the challenges and uncertainties that traders may encounter and learn risk management techniques to safeguard capital and ensure resilience in the face of market fluctuations.

This opening chapter sets the stage for your journey toward self-reliance in trading. Whether you are a novice seeking foundational knowledge or an experienced trader aiming to refine your strategies, "Trade Phenomena" provides a comprehensive guide to navigate the diverse landscape of trading strategies. Gain the insights needed to make informed decisions across various time horizons and achieve success in your trading endeavors.

Short-term Trading Strategies:

Delve into the world of short-term trading strategies in "Trade Phenomena: The Path to Self-Reliance." This section explores dynamic approaches tailored for traders seeking to capitalize on immediate market opportunities and navigate the fast-paced nature of short-term price movements.

❖ **Scalping:**

Embark on the precision-focused strategy of scalping, where traders aim to profit from small price fluctuations within extremely short timeframes. Uncover the techniques used by scalpers to execute swift trades and exploit intraday market dynamics, all while managing risk in a high-speed trading environment.

❖ **Day Trading:**

Explore the art and science of day trading, a strategy where positions are opened and closed within a single trading day. Learn the analytical tools, chart patterns, and risk management principles that empower day traders to make informed decisions in the face of intraday volatility. Understand the significance of timely entries and exits to capture daily market opportunities.

❖ **Range Trading:**

Navigate the market neutrality of range trading, a strategy employed when an asset's price moves within a defined range. Discover how traders identify support and resistance levels to execute buy and sell orders strategically. Explore the nuances of profiting from price oscillations within a specific range while mitigating risks associated with market uncertainty.

Whether you're drawn to the rapid pace of scalping, the daily excitement of day trading, or the strategic patience of range trading, this chapter equips you with insights into short-term trading strategies. "Trade Phenomena" provides practical guidance, dos and don'ts, and a comprehensive understanding of the benefits and risks associated with short-term trading. Elevate your trading acumen and embrace the opportunities that short-term strategies offer in the pursuit of financial self-reliance.

1. Scalping:

Scalping: A Quick Guide

Objective:

Scalping is a short-term trading strategy with the primary goal of capturing small price movements in the market. Traders who employ scalping aim to make quick, small profits by entering and exiting positions rapidly. This strategy requires a high level of precision, discipline, and the ability to react swiftly to changing market conditions.

Key Characteristics:

1. Frequency of Trades:

Scalpers execute a large number of trades within a single day, sometimes even within minutes. The focus is on exploiting minor price fluctuations.

2. Short Holding Period:

Positions are typically held for a very short duration, often just a few seconds to a few minutes. Scalpers aim to capitalize on immediate market inefficiencies.

3. Technical Analysis:

Technical analysis is crucial for scalping. Traders rely on charts, indicators, and patterns to make quick decisions about entry and exit points.

4. Low Profit Margins:

Scalpers target small price movements, aiming for a high volume of trades to accumulate profits. Each trade may yield a small profit, but the cumulative gains can be significant.

5. Tight Stop Loss (SL) and Take Profit (TP) Orders:

Scalpers use tight stop loss orders to limit potential losses and take profit orders to secure small gains quickly. Risk management is a critical aspect of scalping.

6. Liquidity and Volatility:

Scalpers prefer highly liquid markets with tight bidask spreads, as this allows for quick and seamless execution of trades. Volatility is also essential to create trading opportunities.

Execution Tips:

1. Selecting Pairs:

Choose currency pairs or assets with high liquidity and volatility. Major currency pairs like EUR/USD and USD/JPY are often preferred by scalpers.

2. Fast Execution Platforms:

Use trading platforms with fast execution speeds. Delayed execution can significantly impact the success of scalping.

3. Timing:

Scalpers often focus on specific times of the day when markets are most active, such as during overlap periods of major trading sessions.

4. Risk Reward Ratio:

Maintain a favorable risk reward ratio. Since scalping involves small gains, it's essential to keep potential losses well controlled.

5. Stay Informed:

Constantly monitor news and events that may impact the market. Unexpected announcements can lead to rapid price movements.

Challenges and Risks:

1. Transaction Costs:

The frequency of trades can result in higher transaction costs, especially if the spread is not favorable.

2. Emotional Discipline:

Scalping demands, a high level of emotional discipline. Rapid decisionmaking and executing trades without hesitation are crucial.

3. Market Noise:

Short-term price movements can be influenced by market noise, making it challenging to distinguish between meaningful trends and random fluctuations.

4. Technology Dependency:

Scalping relies heavily on technology. Technical issues or internet disruptions can have a significant impact on performance.

5. Psychological Stress:

The fastpaced nature of scalping can be mentally taxing. Traders need to manage stress and avoid burnout.

Conclusion:

Scalping is a trading strategy suited for individuals who thrive in a fastpaced environment and can make quick decisions. Successful scalping requires a solid understanding of technical analysis, effective risk management, and the ability to maintain emotional discipline in the face of rapid market changes. It is not recommended for beginners or those who are not comfortable with the inherent challenges and risks.

Scalping: Dos and Don'ts, Benefits and Risks

Dos:

1. Utilize Tight Risk Management:
Do: Set tight stop loss orders to limit potential losses. Since scalping involves small profit margins, effective risk management is crucial.

2. Focus on Highly Liquid Assets:
Do: Trade in highly liquid markets with tight bidask spreads. This ensures that orders can be executed quickly and with minimal slippage.

3. Use Fast Execution Platforms:
Do: Choose trading platforms with fast execution speeds. Quick and seamless order execution is essential for successful scalping.

4. Stay Informed about Market Conditions:
Do: Constantly monitor market news and events that may impact the assets you are trading. Be aware of economic releases and other factors influencing volatility.

5. Select the Right Timeframes:
Do: Choose shorter timeframes for analysis, such as one or fiveminute charts. Scalpers need to act quickly, and shorter timeframes provide a more immediate view of market movements.

Don'ts:

1. Avoid Neglecting Transaction Costs:
Don't: Overlook transaction costs. With the high frequency of trades in scalping, transaction costs can accumulate. Factor these costs into your overall strategy.

2. Don't Chase the Market:
Don't: Chase the market or try to recover losses quickly. Stick to your predefined trading plan and avoid impulsive decisionmaking.

3. Avoid Overleveraging:
Don't: Overleveraged your positions. While leverage can amplify profits, it also increases the risk of significant losses. Keep leverage within manageable levels.

4. Don't Trade During Low Volatility:
Don't: Engage in scalping during periods of low market volatility. Scalping relies on price movements, and low volatility may result in minimal trading opportunities.

5. Avoid Ignoring Fundamental Factors:
Don't: Completely ignore fundamental factors. While technical analysis is essential in scalping, staying aware of broader market trends and economic developments is still important.

Benefits:

1. Quick Profits:

Scalping allows for the potential of quick, small profits, contributing to the cumulative gains over a series of trades.

2. Adaptability:

Scalping is adaptable to different market conditions. Traders can adjust their strategies to changing trends and capitalize on shortterm opportunities.

3. Reduced Overnight Risk:

Since scalpers typically close positions within the same day, they are not exposed to overnight market risk.

Risks:

1. Transaction Costs:

The frequency of trades in scalping can lead to higher transaction costs, impacting overall profitability.

2. Emotional Stress:

The fastpaced nature of scalping can be mentally challenging, leading to stress and fatigue.

3. Technology Dependency:

Scalping heavily relies on technology. Technical issues or disruptions can result in missed opportunities or execution errors.

4. Limited Profit Margins:

While the frequency of trades can contribute to cumulative profits, each individual trade's profit margin is generally small.

5. Market Noise:

Shortterm price movements can be influenced by market noise, making it challenging to distinguish between meaningful trends and random fluctuations.

Scalping is a trading strategy that requires a specific skill set, including quick decisionmaking, discipline, and the ability to manage stress. Traders should carefully consider the dos and don'ts, weigh the benefits against the risks, and be aware of the challenges associated with this highspeed trading approach.

2. Day Trading:

Day Trading: A Comprehensive Guide

Objective:

Day trading is a shortterm trading strategy where traders aim to capitalize on intraday price movements. The primary objective is to execute multiple trades within a single trading day, closing all positions before the market closes. Day traders seek to profit from shortterm volatility, utilizing various technical analysis tools.

Key Characteristics:

1. Intraday Focus:

Day trading involves entering and exiting positions within the same trading day, avoiding overnight exposure to market risks.

2. Technical Analysis Emphasis:

Traders rely heavily on technical analysis, studying charts, indicators, and patterns to make informed decisions.

3. High Trade Frequency:

Day traders execute numerous trades in a single day, taking advantage of small price movements to accumulate profits.

4. Risk Management:

Effective risk management is crucial. Day traders often use stoploss orders to limit potential losses and set profit targets.

5. Quick DecisionMaking:

Day traders need to make rapid decisions based on realtime market information. Analyzing and executing trades promptly is essential.

Execution Tips:

1. Selecting Tradable Assets:

Choose assets with high liquidity and volatility, such as major currency pairs, stocks, or indices.

2. Technical Analysis Tools:

Utilize technical indicators (RSI, MACD, moving averages) and chart patterns to identify potential entry and exit points.

3. Stay Informed:

Keep abreast of market news, economic releases, and other factors that may impact intraday price movements.

4. Premarket and Aftermarket Analysis:

Analyze premarket and aftermarket price movements to anticipate potential market directions at the opening bell.

5. RiskReward Ratios:

Maintain a favorable riskreward ratio for each trade. Assess potential losses against potential gains before entering a position.

Challenges and Risks:

1. Emotional Discipline:

The fastpaced nature of day trading can evoke emotions. Maintaining emotional discipline and sticking to a trading plan is crucial.

2. Transaction Costs:

Frequent trading can lead to higher transaction costs. Traders need to consider commissions, fees, and bidask spreads.

3. Overtrading:

The temptation to overtrade can be high. Traders should focus on quality setups and avoid excessive trading activity.

4. Market Noise:

Intraday price movements can be influenced by market noise. Distinguishing between noise and meaningful trends is a challenge.

5. Technology Dependence:

Reliable and fast technology is essential. Technical issues or internet disruptions can result in missed opportunities or execution errors.

Benefits:

1. Quick Profits:

Day traders aim to profit from shortterm price movements, providing opportunities for quick gains.

2. Reduced Overnight Risk:

By closing all positions before the market closes, day traders avoid overnight exposure to potential market gaps or news events.

3. Adaptability:

Day traders can adapt to changing market conditions and capitalize on intraday trends or reversals.

Risks:

1. Emotional Stress:

The intensity of intraday trading can lead to emotional stress. Maintaining a calm and disciplined approach is essential.

2. TimeConsuming:

Day trading requires significant time and attention, making it challenging for those with other commitments.

3. Limited Profit Margins:

While individual trades may provide quick profits, the profit margins per trade can be relatively small.

Day Trading: Dos and Don'ts for Successful Strategies

Day trading is a shortterm trading strategy where traders aim to profit from intraday price movements. Here are dos and don'ts to consider when implementing day trading strategies:

Dos:

1. Create a Trading Plan:

Do: Develop a detailed trading plan that includes your trading goals, risk tolerance, and strategies. A plan helps you stay disciplined and focused during fastpaced market conditions.

2. Use Technical Analysis:

Do: Rely on technical analysis tools, charts, and indicators for decisionmaking. Analyzing price patterns, trends, and key technical indicators is essential for identifying potential entry and exit points.

3. Set Realistic Goals:

Do: Set realistic daily and weekly trading goals. Establishing achievable targets helps you maintain focus and avoid excessive risktaking to meet unrealistic expectations.

4. Manage Risk:

Do: Implement strict risk management practices. Set stoploss orders to limit potential losses and use position sizing based on your risk tolerance to avoid overexposure.

5. Stay Informed About Market News:

Do: Stay informed about market news and economic events that could impact the assets you are trading. Realtime information is crucial for making informed decisions in a dynamic market.

6. Adapt to Market Conditions:

Do: Be adaptable to changing market conditions. Day traders should be ready to adjust their strategies based on volatility, liquidity, and other factors influencing the market.

7. Practice with a Demo Account:

Do: Practice your day trading strategies with a demo account before risking real capital. This allows you to refine your approach and gain confidence in your abilities.

Don'ts:

1. Trade Without a Plan:

Don't: Engage in day trading without a welldefined plan. Having a structured plan helps you make rational decisions and avoids impulsive trading.

2. Overtrade:

Don't: Overtrade by taking excessive positions or making too many trades in a single day. Quality over quantity is essential in day trading.

3. Ignore RiskReward Ratios:

Don't: Ignore riskreward ratios. Each trade should have a clear riskreward profile, ensuring that potential profits justify the level of risk taken.

4. Hold Losing Positions:

Don't: Hold onto losing positions hoping for a reversal. Cut losses quickly according to your predetermined risk management strategy.

5. Trade Based on Emotions:

Don't: Let emotions dictate your trading decisions. Fear and greed can lead to impulsive actions, and it's crucial to stick to your predetermined plan.

6. Neglect Technical Analysis:

Don't: Neglect the importance of technical analysis. Day trading relies heavily on charts and indicators for making splitsecond decisions.

7. Trade During Low Liquidity Periods:

Don't: Trade during low liquidity periods when spreads may be wider, and price movements can be more erratic. Stick to the most liquid trading hours for your chosen assets.

Day trading requires a combination of skill, discipline, and adaptability. By following these dos and don'ts, day traders can increase their chances of success in the fastpaced environment of intraday trading. Always remember that day trading involves significant risks, and thorough preparation is essential for minimizing potential losses.

3. Range Trading:

Range Trading: A Comprehensive Guide
Objective:

Range trading is a strategy where traders aim to profit from the price movements within a welldefined range. The primary objective is to identify key support and resistance levels and execute trades at these boundaries. Range traders capitalize on the predictability of price movements within a range by buying at support and selling at resistance.

Key Characteristics:

1. Identifying Support and Resistance:

Range traders focus on identifying clear support and resistance levels on price charts.

2. Horizontal Price Movements:

The price typically moves horizontally within the established range. Range traders aim to capture profits by trading within these horizontal boundaries.

3. Technical Analysis Emphasis:

Technical analysis plays a crucial role in range trading. Traders use indicators, chart patterns, and trendlines to identify potential entry and exit points.

4. Short to MediumTerm Strategy:

Range trading is often executed over shorter to mediumterm timeframes. Positions are typically held for a few days to a few weeks.

5. Risk Management:

Effective risk management is essential. Range traders use stoploss orders to limit potential losses and set profit targets within the established range.

Execution Tips:

1. Identify Clear Ranges:

Look for markets or assets that exhibit welldefined ranges. Analyze historical price movements to identify key support and resistance levels.

2. Use Technical Indicators:

Apply technical indicators, such as moving averages or oscillators, to confirm potential entry and exit points within the range.

3. Wait for Confirmation:

Wait for confirmation of a bounce off support or a retreat from resistance before entering a trade. Avoid preemptive entries.

4. Implement RiskReward Ratios:

Maintain a favorable riskreward ratio for each trade. Assess potential losses against potential gains before entering a position.

5. Stay Informed about Market Conditions:

Keep abreast of market news and events that may impact the established range. Be prepared to adjust your strategy based on changing conditions.

Challenges and Risks:

1. Market Breakouts:

Ranges can be broken, leading to unexpected price movements. Traders should be prepared to adapt their strategies if a breakout occurs.

2. Market Noise:

Shortterm market noise can lead to false breakouts or breakdowns within the range, challenging the accuracy of entry and exit points.

3. Trend Reversals:

Sudden trend reversals outside the established range can catch range traders off guard. Monitoring broader market trends is important.

4. Psychological Discipline:

Maintaining discipline is crucial. Range traders should avoid making impulsive decisions and stick to their predefined trading plan.

Benefits:

1. Predictable Price Movements:

Range trading capitalizes on the predictability of price movements within a welldefined range, providing a structured trading environment.

2. Risk Management:

With clear support and resistance levels, range traders can implement effective risk management strategies, limiting potential losses.

3. Adaptability:

Range trading is adaptable to different market conditions, providing opportunities to profit in both trending and ranging markets.

Risks:

1. Sudden Breakouts:

Unexpected breakouts or breakdowns from the established range can result in significant losses for range traders.

2. Market Noise:

Shortterm fluctuations and noise within the range can lead to false signals, impacting the accuracy of trades.

3. Limited Profit Margins:

While range trading provides a structured approach, profit margins per trade may be relatively small.

Range Trading: Dos and Don'ts for Successful Strategies

Range trading is a strategy that involves identifying price ranges and trading within those boundaries. Here are dos and don'ts to consider when implementing range trading strategies:

Dos:

1. Identify Clear Support and Resistance Levels:

Do: Thoroughly analyze historical price data to identify clear support and resistance levels. These levels define the trading range and provide guidance for entry and exit points.

2. Use Technical Indicators:

Do: Utilize technical indicators such as Bollinger Bands, Moving Averages, or the Relative Strength Index (RSI) to confirm potential reversal points within the identified range.

3. Wait for Confirmation:

Do: Wait for confirmation before entering a trade. Look for price action signals, such as candlestick patterns or trend reversals, that validate the likelihood of the range continuing.

4. Implement RiskReward Ratios:

Do: Use riskreward ratios to assess the potential gain against the potential loss before entering a trade. This ensures that the potential reward justifies the risk taken.

5. Stay Informed About Market Conditions:

Do: Stay informed about market news and events that may impact the trading range. External factors can influence price movements, so being aware of market conditions is essential.

6. Set Clear StopLoss and TakeProfit Levels:

Do: Set clear stoploss and takeprofit levels to manage risk. Having predefined exit points helps discipline and ensures that emotions don't drive trading decisions.

7. Adapt to Changing Market Conditions:

Do: Be adaptable to changing market conditions. If the range starts to break down or if volatility increases, adjust your strategy accordingly.

Don'ts:

1. Trade in Low Volatility Environments:

Don't: Avoid trading in low volatility environments where price movements are minimal. Range trading relies on price oscillations within a defined range, and low volatility may result in less profitable trades.

2. Ignore Fundamental Analysis:

Don't: While range trading is primarily a technical analysis strategy, don't completely ignore fundamental analysis. Major news events or economic releases can impact price movements, even within a range.

3. Force Trades Outside the Range:

Don't: Resist the temptation to force trades outside the established range. Range trading is about capitalizing on price oscillations within the defined boundaries, and attempting trades beyond the range can increase risk.

4. Neglect Risk Management:

Don't: Neglect risk management. Establishing a riskreward ratio, setting stoploss orders, and managing position sizes are crucial components of a successful range trading strategy.

5. Overlook Confirmation Signals:

Don't: Enter trades without waiting for confirmation signals. Relying solely on gut feelings or making impulsive decisions can lead to losses.

6. Become Overly Complacent:

Don't: Become overly complacent during stable market conditions. While range trading can be effective, markets can change, and staying vigilant is essential.

7. Forget to Review and Adjust:

Don't: Forget to regularly review your range trading strategy and adjust it as needed. Markets evolve, and what works well in one period may need modifications in another.

Range trading can be a profitable strategy when executed with discipline and a clear understanding of market conditions. By following these dos and don'ts, traders can enhance their range trading approach and improve the likelihood of success within the identified price boundaries.

Medium-term Trading Strategies:

Delve into the realm of medium-term trading strategies, a balanced approach that combines the agility of short-term trading with the broader perspective required for long-term success. In this segment of "Trade Phenomena: The Path to Self-Reliance," we explore three prominent techniques tailored for the medium-term horizon.

❖ Swing Trading:

Embark on a journey through the dynamic landscape of swing trading. Discover how swing traders leverage short to medium-term price swings within an overarching trend. Uncover the art of identifying entry and exit points based on price patterns, technical indicators, and market momentum. Gain insights into the flexibility and adaptability that characterize successful swing trading strategies.

❖ Trend Following:

Immerse yourself in the strategy of trend following, a medium-term approach designed to capture sustained price movements. Explore the principles of identifying and riding trends, utilizing technical analysis tools to align with the prevailing market direction. Understand the nuances of trend identification, confirmation, and potential reversal points, empowering you to navigate the markets with confidence.

❖ Breakout Trading:

Unlock the potential of breakout trading, a strategy focused on identifying key price levels where a financial instrument could experience a significant price movement. Delve into the principles of recognizing breakout patterns, understanding volatility, and executing trades when markets breach established support or resistance levels. Learn how breakout trading aligns with medium-term goals, providing opportunities for capitalizing on emerging trends.

This section equips traders and investors with the knowledge and skills needed to navigate the complexities of medium-term trading. Whether you are seeking to capture shorter trends or participate in more extended market movements, the strategies explored in "Trade Phenomena" provide a comprehensive guide to effective decision-making and success in the medium-term trading landscape.

1. Swing Trading:

Swing Trading: A Comprehensive Guide

Objective:

Swing trading is a strategy that aims to capture price "swings" within a trend. Traders who engage in swing trading typically hold positions for a few days to weeks, taking advantage of shorttomediumterm price movements. The objective is to enter trades at key support or resistance levels and profit from the expected price changes within the overall trend.

Key Characteristics:

1. Medium-term Timeframe:

Swing trading operates within a medium-term timeframe, with positions typically held for several days to a few weeks.

2. Trend Identification:

Traders focus on identifying and trading within the prevailing trend. They seek to capture price swings that occur as the market moves in the direction of the overall trend.

3. Technical Analysis Emphasis:

Swing traders heavily rely on technical analysis, using tools such as trendlines, moving averages, and chart patterns to identify potential entry and exit points.

4. Risk Management:

Effective risk management is crucial. Swing traders use stoploss orders and set profit targets to manage their trades within the context of the overall trend.

5. Market Sentiment Awareness:

Swing traders are aware of market sentiment and news that may impact the overall trend. They adjust their strategies based on evolving market conditions.

Execution Tips:

1. Identify Trends:

Determine the prevailing trend by analyzing price charts. Look for higher highs and higher lows in an uptrend, and lower highs and lower lows in a downtrend.

2. Use Technical Indicators:

Apply technical indicators, such as moving averages, RSI, or MACD, to confirm trend direction and potential entry points.

3. Wait for Confirmations:

Wait for confirmation of trend reversals or bounces before entering a trade. Patience is crucial in swing trading.

4. Implement RiskReward Ratios:

Maintain a favorable riskreward ratio for each trade. Assess potential losses against potential gains before entering a position.

5. Stay Informed about Market Conditions:

Keep abreast of market news and events that may impact the overall trend. Be prepared to adjust your strategy based on changing conditions.

Challenges and Risks:

1. Trend Reversals:

Swing traders may face challenges when trends suddenly reverse. Adequate risk management is essential to mitigate potential losses.

2. Market Noise:

Short-term market noise or minor corrections within the overall trend can lead to false signals, impacting the accuracy of trades.

3. Overnight Risk:

Unlike day traders, swing traders hold positions overnight, exposing them to potential gaps in the market due to overnight news or events.

4. Psychological Discipline:

Swing traders need to maintain emotional discipline and avoid making impulsive decisions, especially during periods of heightened market volatility.

Benefits:

1. Profit from Trends:

Swing trading allows traders to profit from the overall direction of the market trends, capturing price swings within the broader movement.

2. Adaptability:

Swing trading is adaptable to different market conditions, providing opportunities to profit in both trending and ranging markets.

3. Reduced Time Commitment:

Unlike day trading, swing trading requires less time commitment, making it suitable for individuals with other obligations.

Risks:

1. Trend Reversals:

Unexpected trend reversals can lead to losses if not identified and managed effectively.

2. Market Noise:

Short-term fluctuations within the trend may result in false signals, impacting the accuracy of trades.

3. Overnight Risk:

Holding positions overnight exposes swing traders to potential gaps in the market.

Dos and Don'ts for Successful Strategies

Swing trading is a strategy that seeks to capture short to medium-term price movements within a larger trend. Here are dos and don'ts to consider when implementing swing trading strategies:

Dos:

1. Identify Clear Trends:

Do: Identify clear trends in the market before initiating swing trades. Understanding the broader trend provides context and increases the probability of successful trades.

2. Use Technical Analysis:

Do: Utilize technical analysis tools and indicators, such as moving averages, trendlines, and oscillators, to identify potential entry and exit points. Technical analysis is crucial for timing swing trades.

3. Set Realistic Price Targets:

Do: Set realistic price targets based on technical analysis and the potential for the stock or asset to move within the identified trend. Having predefined targets helps in making disciplined trading decisions.

4. Implement Risk Management:

Do: Implement sound risk management practices. Set stoploss orders to limit potential losses and adhere to a riskreward ratio that justifies the risk taken on each trade.

5. Consider Volume Analysis:

Do: Consider analyzing trading volume when making swing trading decisions. Volume can provide insights into the strength of a price movement and the potential sustainability of the trend.

6. Stay Informed About Market Catalysts:

Do: Stay informed about market catalysts and events that could impact the stocks or assets you are trading. External factors, such as earnings reports or economic data releases, can influence price movements.

7. Adapt to Changing Market Conditions:

Do: Be adaptable to changing market conditions. Market dynamics can shift, and staying flexible allows you to adjust your strategy accordingly.

Don'ts:

1. Ignore the Larger Trend:

Don't: Ignore the larger trend in the market. While swing trading focuses on shorterterm movements, it's essential to be aware of the overall market direction to align trades with the broader trend.

2. Neglect Technical Analysis:

Don't: Neglect the importance of technical analysis. Detailed chart analysis, trend identification, and using technical indicators are essential for effective swing trading.

3. Chase the Market:

Don't: Chase the market or enter trades impulsively. Wait for confirmation signals and ensure that your entry points align with your analysis and strategy.

4. Overlook Fundamental Factors:

Don't: Overlook fundamental factors entirely. While swing trading is primarily based on technical analysis, being aware of relevant fundamental factors can provide a more comprehensive view.

5. Disregard RiskReward Ratios:

Don't: Disregard riskreward ratios. Each trade should have a clear riskreward profile, ensuring that potential profits justify the level of risk taken.

6. Trade Without a Plan:

Don't: Trade without a welldefined plan. Having a trading plan that outlines entry and exit points, risk management strategies, and criteria for trade selection is crucial for success.

7. Hold Positions During Major News:

Don't: Hold swing trading positions during major news events or earnings releases. Volatility during such events can lead to unexpected price movements, and it's often prudent to exit positions beforehand.

Swing trading requires a combination of technical analysis, risk management, and adaptability. By following these dos and don'ts, traders can enhance their swing trading strategies and increase the likelihood of successful trades within the short to mediumterm price movements.

2. Trend Following:

Trend Following: A Comprehensive Guide

Objective:

Trend following is a trading strategy that aims to capitalize on sustained price movements in the market. Traders employing this strategy identify and follow established trends, seeking to profit from the momentum of the market. The objective is to enter positions in the direction of the prevailing trend and ride the trend until signs of a reversal emerge.

Key Characteristics:

1. Trend Identification:

Trendfollowing traders focus on identifying and trading in the direction of established trends. This can be an uptrend (higher highs and higher lows) or a downtrend (lower highs and lower lows).

2. Technical Analysis Emphasis:

Technical analysis plays a crucial role in trend following. Traders use indicators, moving averages, trendlines, and other tools to identify and confirm trends.

3. Medium to LongTerm Timeframe:

Trendfollowing strategies are often implemented over medium to longterm timeframes. Positions may be held for weeks, months, or even longer.

4. Risk Management:

Effective risk management is crucial. Trend followers use stoploss orders and other risk mitigation techniques to protect capital.

5. Market Sentiment Awareness:

Trend followers are aware of broader market sentiment and major economic factors that may influence the overall trend. They adjust their strategies based on evolving market conditions.

Execution Tips:

1. Identify Trends:

Determine the prevailing trend by analyzing price charts. Trendfollowing traders look for clear and sustained directional movements.

2. Use Trend Indicators:

Apply trendfollowing indicators, such as moving averages, to confirm trend direction and potential entry points.

3. Wait for Trend Confirmation:

Wait for confirmation of a sustained trend before entering a trade. Patience is a key attribute of trendfollowing strategies.

4. Implement RiskReward Ratios:

Maintain a favorable riskreward ratio for each trade. Assess potential losses against potential gains before entering a position.

5. Stay Informed about Market Conditions:

Keep abreast of market news and events that may impact the established trend. Be prepared to adjust your strategy based on changing conditions.

Challenges and Risks:

1. Trend Reversals:

Trend followers may face challenges when trends suddenly reverse. Adequate risk management is essential to mitigate potential losses.

2. False Signals:

Shortterm fluctuations or noise within the overall trend can result in false signals, impacting the accuracy of trades.

3. Overnight Risk:

Holding positions overnight exposes trend followers to potential gaps in the market due to overnight news or events.

4. Psychological Discipline:

Maintaining emotional discipline is crucial for trend followers, especially during periods of market volatility or when trends encounter temporary setbacks.

Benefits:

1. Profit from Sustained Trends:

Trend following allows traders to profit from sustained directional movements in the market.

2. Adaptability:

Trendfollowing strategies can be adaptable to different timeframes and market conditions.

3. Reduced Time Commitment:

Depending on the specific approach, trend following may require less time commitment compared to day trading.

Risks:

1. Trend Reversals:

Unexpected trend reversals can lead to losses if not identified and managed effectively.

2. False Signals:

Shortterm fluctuations within the trend may result in false signals, impacting the accuracy of trades.

3. Overnight Risk:

Holding positions overnight exposes trend followers to potential gaps in the market.

Dos and Don'ts for Successful Strategies

Trend following is a trading strategy that aims to capture gains by riding the prevailing market trend. Here are dos and don'ts to consider when implementing trendfollowing strategies:

Dos:

1. Identify Clear Trends:

Do: Identify clear and wellestablished trends in the market. Look for sustained upward (bullish) or downward (bearish) movements in prices before considering trendfollowing strategies.

2. Use Trend Indicators:

Do: Utilize trend indicators such as Moving Averages, trendlines, or trend channels to identify the direction of the trend. These tools can help you confirm the existence of a trend and provide entry and exit signals.

3. Set Clear Entry and Exit Points:

Do: Define clear entry and exit points based on the trend. Establish specific criteria for entering a trade when a trend is identified and determine conditions for exiting to capture profits or limit losses.

4. Implement Risk Management:

Do: Implement effective risk management practices. Set stoploss orders to limit potential losses and use position sizing to ensure that your exposure aligns with your risk tolerance.

5. Stay Informed About Market Conditions:

Do: Stay informed about market news and events that could impact the overall trend. While trendfollowing is primarily technical, external factors can influence market dynamics.

6. Adapt to Changing Trends:

Do: Be adaptable to changing trends. Markets can shift, and trendfollowing strategies should allow for adjustments to new conditions.

7. Diversify Your Assets:

Do: Diversify your assets when trendfollowing. Apply the strategy across different markets or assets to reduce the impact of poor performance in a specific sector.

Don'ts:

1. Trade Against the Trend:

Don't: Trade against the trend. Trendfollowing strategies are designed to capitalize on existing trends, and attempting to trade against the prevailing direction can increase the risk of losses.

2. Ignore Conflicting Signals:

Don't: Ignore conflicting signals from different indicators. Analyze multiple indicators to confirm the strength of the trend and avoid relying solely on a single signal.

3. Overlook Historical Price Action:

Don't: Overlook historical price action. Analyzing past price movements can provide insights into how trends have behaved in similar situations, helping in making informed decisions.

4. Neglect Fundamental Factors:

Don't: Neglect fundamental factors entirely. While trend following is primarily based on technical analysis, being aware of relevant fundamental factors can provide a more comprehensive view.

5. Chase the Market:

Don't: Chase the market or enter trades impulsively. Wait for confirmation signals and ensure that your entry points align with the established trend.

6. Rely Solely on Indicators:

Don't: Rely solely on indicators without considering broader market conditions. Context is crucial, and understanding the overall market environment enhances the effectiveness of trendfollowing strategies.

7. Hold Positions Indefinitely:

Don't: Hold onto trendfollowing positions indefinitely. Have a predefined exit strategy to lock in profits and manage risks.

Trend following can be a powerful strategy when implemented with discipline and a thorough understanding of market conditions. By following these dos and don'ts, traders can enhance their trendfollowing approach and increase the likelihood of success in capturing profits during sustained market trends.

3. Breakout Trading:

Breakout Trading: A Comprehensive Guide

Objective:

Breakout trading is a strategy that aims to capitalize on significant price movements occurring after an asset's price breaks through a key support or resistance level. Traders employing this strategy seek to enter positions as the price "breaks out" from a welldefined range or chart pattern, anticipating that the breakout will lead to a sustained directional movement.

Key Characteristics:

1. Identifying Key Levels:

Breakout traders focus on identifying key support or resistance levels, trendlines, or chart patterns where a breakout is likely to occur.

2. Volatility Emphasis:

Breakout trading is often associated with increased volatility. Traders seek assets with potential for substantial price movements.

3. Technical Analysis Emphasis:

Technical analysis plays a crucial role in breakout trading. Traders use indicators, chart patterns, and trendlines to identify potential breakout points.

4. Short to MediumTerm Timeframe:

Breakout trades are often executed over short to mediumterm timeframes, capturing the initial momentum following the breakout.

5. Risk Management:

Effective risk management is crucial. Breakout traders use stoploss orders and other risk mitigation techniques to protect capital.

Execution Tips:

1. Identify Potential Breakout Levels:

Analyze historical price movements to identify potential breakout levels. Look for patterns like triangles, rectangles, or head and shoulders that indicate a possible breakout.

2. Confirm Breakouts:

Wait for confirmation of a breakout by observing increased volume and a decisive move beyond the key level. False breakouts can occur, so confirmation is essential.

3. Use Technical Indicators:

Utilize technical indicators such as Bollinger Bands, RSI, or MACD to confirm potential breakout signals.

4. Implement RiskReward Ratios:

Maintain a favorable riskreward ratio for each trade. Assess potential losses against potential gains before entering a breakout position.

5. Stay Informed about Market Conditions:

Keep abreast of market news and events that may impact the asset's potential breakout. Be prepared to adjust your strategy based on changing conditions.

Challenges and Risks:

1. False Breakouts:

One of the primary challenges is dealing with false breakouts, where the price briefly moves beyond a key level before reverting.

2. Whipsaw Movements:

Whipsaw movements, characterized by sudden reversals after a breakout, can lead to losses for breakout traders.

3. Overtrading:

The anticipation of potential breakouts may lead to overtrading, which can increase transaction costs and impact overall profitability.

4. Psychological Discipline:

Maintaining emotional discipline is crucial for breakout traders, especially during periods of market volatility or when dealing with false signals.

Benefits:

1. Capturing Strong Trends:

Breakout trading allows traders to capture strong trends and capitalize on the momentum generated by the breakout.

2. Quick Profits:

Successful breakout trades can result in quick profits, especially if the asset experiences a rapid and sustained directional movement.

3. Adaptability:

Breakout trading can be adaptable to different timeframes and market conditions.

Risks:

1. False Breakouts:

Dealing with false breakouts can lead to losses if not identified and managed effectively.

2. Whipsaw Movements:

Sudden reversals after a breakout can result in losses for traders caught on the wrong side of the market.

3. Overtrading:

Overtrading can lead to increased transaction costs and may impact overall profitability.

Dos and Don'ts for Successful Strategies

Breakout trading is a strategy that involves entering a trade when an asset's price breaks through a significant level of support or resistance. Here are dos and don'ts to consider when implementing breakout trading strategies:

Dos:

1. Identify Strong Support or Resistance Levels:

Do: Identify welldefined and strong support or resistance levels. Breakout trades are most effective when there is a clear and significant level that the price is breaking through.

2. Use Confirmation Indicators:

Do: Use confirmation indicators, such as volume or other technical indicators, to validate the breakout. Confirming signals can increase the reliability of the breakout and reduce false signals.

3. Wait for Confirmation:

Do: Wait for confirmation of the breakout before entering a trade. Confirming the breakout helps avoid false signals and ensures that the price is genuinely moving in the expected direction.

4. Implement Risk Management:

Do: Implement sound risk management practices. Set stoploss orders to limit potential losses and determine position sizes based on your risk tolerance.

5. Consider Time of Day:

Do: Consider the time of day when trading breakouts. Breakouts during higher volume periods, such as the opening hours of major markets, may have more significant followthrough.

6. Stay Informed About Market Conditions:

Do: Stay informed about market news and events that could impact the breakout. External factors can influence price movements, so being aware of market conditions is essential.

7. Adapt to Changing Conditions:

Do: Be adaptable to changing market conditions. If a breakout fails or if the market dynamics shift, adjust your strategy accordingly.

Don'ts:

1. Ignore False Breakouts:

Don't: Ignore false breakouts. False breakouts can lead to losses, and it's crucial to have mechanisms in place, such as stoploss orders, to limit the impact of trades that do not follow through.

2. Trade Without Confirmation:

Don't: Trade without waiting for confirmation of the breakout. Impulsive trading without confirming signals can lead to entering trades prematurely.

3. Neglect Volume Analysis:

Don't: Neglect the analysis of trading volume. Volume can provide insights into the strength of a breakout, and confirming a breakout with significant volume can increase the confidence in the trade.

4. Ignore Overall Market Trends:

Don't: Ignore the overall market trends. While breakout trading focuses on shortterm price movements, understanding the broader trend can provide context and increase the likelihood of successful breakouts.

5. Disregard RiskReward Ratios:

Don't: Disregard riskreward ratios. Each breakout trade should have a clear riskreward profile, ensuring that potential profits justify the level of risk taken.

6. Trade Illiquid Assets:

Don't: Trade illiquid assets. Low liquidity can result in erratic price movements, slippage, and difficulties in executing trades at desired levels.

7. Hold Onto Losing Positions:

Don't: Hold onto losing breakout positions hoping for a reversal. Implementing strict stoploss orders is essential to manage risk and avoid significant losses.

Breakout trading can be a profitable strategy when executed with discipline and a clear understanding of market conditions. By following these dos and don'ts, traders can enhance their breakout trading approach and improve the likelihood of successful trades when assets break through significant support or resistance levels.

Long-term Investment Strategies:

In the expansive landscape of long-term investment strategies, the chapter "Trading Strategies" within "Trade Phenomena: The Path to Self-Reliance" delves into enduring approaches that transcend the frenetic pace of daily market fluctuations. This section focuses on three prominent strategies tailored for investors with a patient outlook and a commitment to wealth accumulation over time.

❖ Hodling:

At the heart of long-term investing, "Hodling" represents a steadfast commitment to holding assets through market fluctuations. Explore the philosophy of weathering short-term volatility with the belief in the fundamental value and future potential of the chosen assets. Gain insights into the art of strategic patience and the potential benefits of riding out market cycles for substantial returns.

❖ Value Investing:

Dive into the principles of "Value Investing," a strategy popularized by renowned investors like Benjamin Graham and Warren Buffett. Learn how to identify undervalued assets in the market and make informed investment decisions based on a thorough analysis of a company's intrinsic value. Uncover the time-tested techniques that value investors employ to seek out opportunities for long-term wealth creation.

❖ Dividend Investing:

Explore the concept of "Dividend Investing" as a cornerstone of long-term financial success. Understand how this strategy involves strategically selecting dividend-paying stocks to generate a steady stream of passive income. Delve into the benefits of receiving regular dividends while maintaining the potential for capital appreciation over the years.

❖ Key Points Covered:

Philosophy of Long-Term Growth: Discover the underlying philosophy that ties these long-term investment strategies together – the pursuit of sustained growth and wealth accumulation over an extended period.

Risk and Reward Balance: Gain insights into how these strategies strike a balance between risk and reward, emphasizing the importance of risk management and capital preservation in the pursuit of long-term financial goals.

Adaptability: Understand the adaptability of these strategies to different market conditions and economic cycles, providing investors with tools to navigate changing landscapes while maintaining a focus on long-term objectives.

❖ Practical Applications:

Building a Diversified Portfolio: Learn how these long-term strategies contribute to the construction of a diversified portfolio that aligns with individual risk tolerance and financial goals.

Investor Mindset: Cultivate the mindset required for successful long-term investing, emphasizing patience, discipline, and a focus on fundamental factors.

In "Trade Phenomena," the exploration of Long-Term Investment Strategies serves as a valuable resource for investors seeking to build wealth steadily over time. Whether you are a seasoned investor or a newcomer to the financial markets, this chapter equips you with the knowledge and strategies needed to navigate the complexities of long-term investing and embark on the path to financial self-reliance.

1. Hodling:

Hodling (Longterm Investing): A Comprehensive Guide

Objective:

Hodling, a term derived from a misspelling of "holding," is a longterm investment strategy where individuals purchase and hold assets with the expectation of substantial price appreciation over an extended period. This approach is often associated with cryptocurrencies, but it can be applied to various asset classes. The primary goal of hodling is to benefit from the longterm growth potential of the chosen investment.

Key Characteristics:

1. Longterm Perspective:

Hodlers adopt a longterm perspective, aiming to hold onto their investments through market fluctuations and shortterm volatility.

2. Fundamental Analysis Emphasis:

Hodling is often based on fundamental analysis, with investors focusing on the intrinsic value and potential of the asset rather than shortterm price movements.

3. Minimal Trading Activity:

Hodlers engage in minimal trading activity, avoiding frequent buying and selling. This strategy is in contrast to shortterm trading approaches.

4. Conviction in the Asset:

Hodlers have strong conviction in the potential of the chosen asset. This belief in the longterm success of the investment often surpasses shortterm market sentiment.

5. Patience and Discipline:

Successful hodling requires patience and discipline. Hodlers are willing to endure market fluctuations and resist the temptation to react to shortterm price changes.

Execution Tips:

1. Choose Fundamentally Strong Assets:

Conduct thorough research and select assets with strong fundamentals and growth potential for longterm hodling.

2. Diversify Portfolio:

Diversification helps spread risk. Hodlers may consider holding a diverse portfolio of assets across different sectors or industries.

3. Ignore Shortterm Volatility:

Hodlers should be prepared to withstand shortterm market volatility and avoid making impulsive decisions based on price fluctuations.

4. Regularly Review Investments:

While hodling involves a longterm perspective, it's essential to periodically review investments and adjust the portfolio based on changing market conditions or the evolution of the asset.

5. Security Measures:

Implement robust security measures, especially in the case of cryptocurrencies. Safeguard private keys and use secure wallets to protect longterm investments.

Challenges and Risks:

1. Market Volatility:

Hodlers must navigate through market volatility and tolerate shortterm price fluctuations without succumbing to panic selling.

2. Asset Specific Risks:

The success of hodling is contingent on the specific asset's performance. External factors, such as regulatory changes or technological developments, can impact the investment.

3. Lack of Liquidity:

Hodling may lead to a lack of liquidity, as assets are held for an extended period. This can limit the ability to capitalize on shortterm market opportunities.

4. Psychological Discipline:

Maintaining psychological discipline is crucial. Hodlers need to overcome the fear of missing out (FOMO) during bullish periods and resist the temptation to sell during downturns.

Benefits:

1. Longterm Growth Potential:

Hodling allows investors to potentially benefit from the longterm growth of fundamentally strong assets.

2. Reduced Transaction Costs:

With minimal trading activity, hodlers may incur fewer transaction costs compared to frequent traders.

3. Capitalizing on Market Trends:

Hodlers capitalize on market trends by staying invested during periods of sustained growth.

Risks:

1. Market Downturns:

Extended market downturns can test the patience and conviction of hodlers, potentially leading to paper losses.

2. Missed Shortterm Opportunities:

Hodlers may miss shortterm profit opportunities that active traders could exploit.

3. Asset Specific Risks:

The success of hodling is dependent on the performance of the selected asset, which may be influenced by various external factors.

Dos and Don'ts for Success

Hodling, a term derived from a misspelling of "hold," represents a longterm investment strategy where investors hold onto their assets through market fluctuations. Here are dos and don'ts for successful hodling:

Dos:

1. Research and Understand Your Investments:

Do: Conduct thorough research on the assets you plan to hodl. Understand the fundamentals, technology, and potential future developments of the projects you're investing in.

2. Diversify Your Portfolio:

Do: Diversify your investment portfolio. Spread your investments across different assets to reduce risk and increase the potential for longterm growth.

3. Have a LongTerm Perspective:

Do: Adopt a longterm perspective. Hodling is based on the belief in the longterm success of your investments, so avoid making decisions based on shortterm market fluctuations.

4. Stay Informed About Market Trends:

Do: Stay informed about market trends and developments in the cryptocurrency and investment space. Awareness of industry changes and advancements can help you make informed decisions.

5. Regularly Review Your Portfolio:

Do: Periodically review your portfolio to ensure it aligns with your longterm goals. Reassess your investments based on changes in market conditions, project developments, and your personal financial situation.

6. Set Realistic Financial Goals:

Do: Set realistic financial goals for your hodling strategy. Understand your investment objectives and what you aim to achieve over the long term.

7. Implement Risk Management:

Do: Implement risk management strategies. This includes setting stoploss levels, diversifying your investments, and having a clear understanding of the risks associated with each asset.

Don'ts:

1. Panic Sell During Market Downturns:

Don't: Panic sell during market downturns. Hodling involves weathering market fluctuations, and selling in a panic can result in realizing losses that might have been avoided by staying the course.

2. Ignore Fundamental Changes:

Don't: Ignore fundamental changes in the projects you're invested in. Stay vigilant about updates, partnerships, and any significant events that may impact the longterm viability of your investments.

3. Chase Shortterm Gains:

Don't: Chase shortterm gains or engage in frequent trading. Hodling is about patience and belief in the longterm potential of your investments.

4. Invest More Than You Can Afford to Lose:

Don't: Invest more than you can afford to lose. While hodling is a longterm strategy, it's essential to consider the possibility of market downturns and only invest what you can afford to hold through volatile periods.

5. Neglect Portfolio Rebalancing:

Don't: Neglect portfolio rebalancing. While hodling involves holding onto assets, it's essential to periodically reassess your portfolio and make adjustments based on changing market conditions.

6. Ignore Market Trends Completely:

Don't: Ignore market trends altogether. While a longterm perspective is crucial, being completely oblivious to market trends and changes can hinder your ability to make informed decisions.

7. Assume All Projects Will Succeed:

Don't: Assume that all projects you invest in will succeed. Perform due diligence, but also acknowledge that not all projects will achieve their goals, and some may face challenges or fail.

Hodling can be a successful strategy when approached with a thoughtful and informed mindset. By following these dos and don'ts, hodlers can navigate the dynamic cryptocurrency market while maintaining a focus on longterm investment goals.

2. Value Investing:

Value Investing: A Comprehensive Guide

Objective:

Value investing is an investment strategy that involves selecting assets, typically stocks, that are believed to be undervalued in the market. The goal of value investing is to buy assets at a price lower than their intrinsic value, anticipating that the market will eventually recognize and correct the undervaluation, leading to capital appreciation.

Key Characteristics:

1. Intrinsic Value Focus:

Value investors emphasize the intrinsic or fundamental value of an asset rather than its market price. They seek to identify discrepancies between intrinsic value and market price.

2. LongTerm Perspective:

Value investing is inherently a longterm strategy. Investors are willing to hold undervalued assets patiently until the market recognizes their true worth.

3. Fundamental Analysis Emphasis:

Fundamental analysis is a cornerstone of value investing. Investors analyze financial statements, earnings reports, and other fundamental indicators to assess the health and potential of a company.

4. Margin of Safety:

Value investors look for a margin of safety, meaning they aim to buy assets at a significant discount to their intrinsic value to provide a buffer against potential uncertainties.

5. Contrarian Approach:

Value investors often adopt a contrarian approach, going against prevailing market sentiment. They may invest in outoffavor or overlooked assets that have the potential for a turnaround.

Execution Tips:

1. Identify Undervalued Assets:

Conduct thorough fundamental analysis to identify assets that are trading below their intrinsic value. Look for factors such as low pricetoearnings ratios, strong balance sheets, and consistent earnings growth.

2. Assess Economic Moats:

Evaluate a company's economic moats, which are competitive advantages that protect it from competition. Companies with sustainable competitive advantages are often favored by value investors.

3. Diversify Portfolio:

Diversification helps spread risk. Value investors may build a diversified portfolio of undervalued assets across different industries to minimize exposure to sectorspecific risks.

4. Monitor for Catalysts:

Keep an eye on potential catalysts that could trigger a reevaluation of the asset by the market. This might include positive changes in management, new product launches, or industry trends.

5. Patience and Discipline:

Successful value investing requires patience. Investors should be prepared to hold undervalued assets for an extended period, allowing time for the market to recognize their true value.

Challenges and Risks:

1. Market Mispricing:

There is a risk that the market might continue to misprice assets, and undervalued investments may take longer to appreciate than anticipated.

2. Value Traps:

Not all undervalued assets will experience a turnaround. Some may be "value traps" with persistent issues that prevent them from realizing their intrinsic value.

3. Economic and Industry Risks:

Economic downturns or industryspecific challenges can impact the performance of value investments, as undervalued assets may struggle in unfavorable economic environments.

4. Psychological Discipline:

Staying disciplined during periods of market volatility and maintaining conviction in undervalued assets can be psychologically challenging.

Benefits:

1. Potential for Capital Appreciation:

Successful value investing can lead to significant capital appreciation as the market recognizes and corrects the undervaluation.

2. Lower Downside Risk:

The focus on intrinsic value and the margin of safety can provide a buffer against downside risks, reducing the likelihood of significant losses.

3. Dividend Income:

Value stocks often pay dividends, providing investors with a potential income stream while they wait for the market to recognize the asset's value.

Risks:

1. Extended Holding Periods:

Value investments may require an extended holding period before their intrinsic value is realized, testing the patience of investors.

2. Market Timing Challenges:

Identifying the optimal entry point for undervalued assets can be challenging, and mistimed investments may not yield the expected returns.

3. Industry and Economic Risks:

Economic downturns or industryspecific challenges can impact the performance of value investments.

Dos and Don'ts for Successful Strategies

Value investing is an investment approach that involves selecting stocks or assets that are believed to be undervalued relative to their intrinsic worth. Here are dos and don'ts to consider when implementing value investing strategies:

Dos:

1. Conduct Thorough Fundamental Analysis:

Do: Conduct indepth fundamental analysis of the companies or assets you are considering for investment. Evaluate financial statements, earnings reports, and other relevant metrics to assess the intrinsic value.

2. Focus on Intrinsic Value:

Do: Focus on the intrinsic value of an investment. Look for opportunities where the market price is below the intrinsic value, indicating potential for longterm capital appreciation.

3. Invest in Strong, Stable Companies:

Do: Invest in companies with strong fundamentals, a history of stable earnings, and a competitive advantage in their industry. Seek businesses with a durable economic moat that can withstand market fluctuations.

4. Have a LongTerm Investment Horizon:

Do: Adopt a longterm investment horizon. Value investing is often most effective when investors have the patience to hold onto undervalued assets until their true worth is recognized by the market.

5. Diversify Your Portfolio:

Do: Diversify your portfolio to spread risk. While value investing focuses on individual assets, having a diversified portfolio helps mitigate the impact of poor performance in any single investment.

6. Seek Margin of Safety:

Do: Seek a margin of safety when investing. Look for assets trading below their intrinsic value, providing a cushion against potential market downturns or miscalculations in valuation.

7. Stay Informed About Economic Trends:

Do: Stay informed about economic trends and industry developments. Understanding the broader economic context helps in making informed decisions about the potential future performance of value investments.

Don'ts:

1. Chase ShortTerm Market Trends:

Don't: Chase shortterm market trends or engage in speculative trading. Value investing is about identifying opportunities based on fundamental analysis, not following shortterm market movements.

2. Ignore Quality of Management:

Don't: Ignore the quality of management. Assess the leadership and governance of the companies you're considering. Competent management is crucial for a company's longterm success.

3. Overlook Debt Levels:

Don't: Overlook the debt levels of potential investments. Excessive debt can pose a risk to a company's financial health, even if other fundamental indicators appear strong.

4. Neglect Regular Portfolio Reviews:

Don't: Neglect regular reviews of your portfolio. Economic conditions and company fundamentals can change, and periodic assessments ensure that your investments continue to align with your strategy.

5. Assume All Undervalued Stocks Will Rebound:

Don't: Assume that all undervalued stocks will rebound. While value investing aims to capitalize on mispriced assets, not every undervalued stock will necessarily experience a significant price increase.

6. Be Impatient with Results:

Don't: Be impatient with results. Value investing may require time for the market to recognize the intrinsic value of an asset. Avoid making impulsive decisions based on shortterm price movements.

7. Neglect Ongoing Research:

Don't: Neglect ongoing research. Stay informed about the companies and industries in which you've invested. Changes in market conditions or the competitive landscape may necessitate adjustments to your portfolio.

Value investing, popularized by renowned investors like Benjamin Graham and Warren Buffett, is a disciplined and patient approach to wealth creation. By adhering to these dos and don'ts, value investors can enhance their ability to identify undervalued opportunities and build a resilient, longterm investment portfolio.

3. Dividend Investing:

Dividend Investing: A Comprehensive Guide

Objective:

Dividend investing is an investment strategy focused on building a portfolio of stocks or other incomegenerating assets that regularly pay dividends to shareholders. The primary objective of dividend investing is to generate a consistent stream of passive income through dividend payouts while potentially benefiting from capital appreciation over the long term.

Key Characteristics:

1. Income Generation:

Dividend investing prioritizes the generation of regular income through dividends, which are typically paid by established and financially stable companies.

2. LongTerm Perspective:

Dividend investors often adopt a longterm perspective, aiming to benefit from both the regular income stream and the potential for the appreciation of the underlying assets.

3. Dividend Yield Consideration:

Investors pay attention to the dividend yield, which is the annual dividend income as a percentage of the investment's current market price. A higher yield may be attractive, but it's important to consider the company's financial health.

4. Stable and Mature Companies:

Dividend investors often prefer stable and mature companies with a history of consistent dividend payments. These companies are perceived as having strong cash flow and financial stability.

5. Reinvestment of Dividends:

Dividend investors may choose to reinvest the dividends received back into additional shares of the same dividendpaying stocks, compounding their investment over time.

Execution Tips:

1. Research Dividend Stocks:

Conduct thorough research to identify dividendpaying stocks. Look for companies with a history of stable dividends, strong financials, and a commitment to shareholder returns.

2. Diversify Portfolio:

Diversification is key to managing risk. Build a diversified portfolio of dividend stocks across different sectors to reduce exposure to industryspecific risks.

3. Consider Dividend Growth:

Some investors focus not only on current dividend yield but also on dividend growth. Companies with a history of increasing dividend payouts may be appealing for longterm investors.

4. Evaluate Payout Ratios:

Assess the payout ratio, which is the proportion of earnings paid out as dividends. A sustainable payout ratio indicates that the company has room to continue paying dividends and potentially increasing them in the future.

5. Monitor for Changes:

Regularly monitor the financial health of the companies in your portfolio. Be aware of any changes in dividend policies, earnings reports, or other factors that may impact dividend payments.

Challenges and Risks:

1. Market Volatility:

Dividend stocks can be sensitive to market fluctuations. Share prices may experience volatility, affecting the overall value of the investment.

2. Economic Downturns:

Economic downturns may impact companies' ability to maintain or increase dividend payouts. Certain sectors may be more vulnerable to economic downturns.

3. Interest Rate Changes:

Changes in interest rates can influence the attractiveness of dividend stocks relative to fixedincome investments. Rising interest rates may lead to shifts in investor preferences.

4. CompanySpecific Risks:

Individual companies may face challenges that affect their ability to pay dividends, such as changes in management, financial difficulties, or shifts in industry dynamics.

Benefits:

1. Steady Income Stream:

Dividend investing provides a steady stream of income through regular dividend payouts, making it attractive for incomeoriented investors.

2. LongTerm Wealth Building:

Reinvesting dividends can contribute to longterm wealth building through the compounding effect, potentially leading to increased capital appreciation.

3. Inflation Hedge:

Dividend income may act as a hedge against inflation, as companies that regularly increase dividends may provide investors with a growing income stream over time.

Risks:

1. Market Volatility:

Dividend stocks may experience price fluctuations, impacting the overall value of the investment.

2. Economic Downturns:

Economic downturns can lead to challenges for companies and affect their ability to maintain or increase dividend payouts.

3. Interest Rate Changes:

Changes in interest rates can influence the relative attractiveness of dividend stocks compared to other investment options.

Dos and Don'ts for Successful Strategies

Dividend investing is an approach that focuses on selecting stocks or assets based on their ability to pay regular dividends. Here are dos and don'ts to consider when implementing dividend investing strategies:

Dos:

1. Research DividendPaying Companies:

Do: Conduct thorough research on companies that have a history of paying consistent and growing dividends. Evaluate their financial health, earnings stability, and dividend payout history.

2. Focus on Dividend Sustainability:

Do: Focus on the sustainability of dividends. Look for companies with a healthy payout ratio (dividends relative to earnings), strong cash flow, and a track record of maintaining or increasing dividend payments over time.

3. Consider Dividend Growth:

Do: Consider companies with a history of growing dividends. Dividend growth indicates that the company is generating sufficient earnings and is committed to returning value to shareholders.

4. Diversify Your Dividend Portfolio:

Do: Diversify your dividend portfolio across different sectors and industries. This helps spread risk and ensures that your income stream is not overly dependent on the performance of a single sector.

5. Reinvest Dividends:

Do: Reinvest dividends to take advantage of compounding. Reinvesting dividends can accelerate the growth of your investment over time.

6. Look for Dividend Aristocrats:

Do: Consider investing in "Dividend Aristocrats" – companies with a history of consistently increasing dividends for at least 25 consecutive years. These companies often demonstrate stability and commitment to shareholder value.

7. Stay Informed About Company Performance:

Do: Stay informed about the financial performance and strategies of the companies in your dividend portfolio. Regularly review earnings reports and updates to ensure that your investments align with your goals.

Don'ts:

1. Chase High Yields Without Caution:

Don't: Chase high dividend yields without considering the underlying fundamentals of the company. Extremely high yields may indicate financial distress or an unsustainable dividend payout.

2. Overlook Dividend Payout Ratios:

Don't: Overlook dividend payout ratios. A high payout ratio may suggest that a company is distributing too much of its earnings as dividends, potentially jeopardizing its ability to invest in growth or navigate challenges.

3. Ignore Changes in Company Health:

Don't: Ignore changes in the health of the company. Economic downturns or shifts in industry dynamics can impact a company's ability to maintain dividend payments.

4. Neglect to Review the Dividend Policy:

Don't: Neglect to review the company's dividend policy. Some companies may have variable dividends, and changes in economic conditions may lead to adjustments or cuts in dividend payouts.

5. Rely Solely on Dividend Yields:

Don't: Rely solely on dividend yields as a metric for investment.

Consider the overall health of the company, its growth prospects, and the sustainability of the dividend.

6. Forget to Reassess Portfolio Regularly:

Don't: Forget to reassess your dividend portfolio regularly. Industries, economic conditions, and company performance can change over time, requiring adjustments to your investment strategy.

7. Assume Past Performance Guarantees Future Results:

Don't: Assume that past dividend performance guarantees future results. While a history of consistent dividends is a positive sign, it's important to continually evaluate the current and future prospects of each investment.

Dividend investing can be a reliable strategy for incomeoriented investors when implemented with care and consideration of the underlying fundamentals. By following these dos and don'ts, investors can build a diversified and resilient dividend portfolio that provides a steady income stream over the long term.

Common Strategies Across All Time Horizons:

Embark on a journey of comprehensive trading strategies that transcend the boundaries of time horizons in "Trade Phenomena: The Path to Self-Reliance." In this segment, we explore the universal principles and techniques that form the backbone of successful trading across different investment timelines.

❖ Risk Management:

Discover the cornerstone of sustainable trading—effective risk management. Regardless of your preferred time horizon, understanding, and implementing sound risk management practices is paramount. Learn how to assess and mitigate potential risks, set appropriate stop-loss levels, and protect your capital in the face of market uncertainties.

❖ Diversification:

Delve into the art of diversification as a key strategy that spans short-term, medium-term, and long-term trading. Uncover the principles of spreading investments across different assets or asset classes to reduce risk exposure. Explore how a well-diversified portfolio can enhance stability, minimize volatility, and contribute to overall long-term success.

❖ Continuous Learning:

Embrace the concept of perpetual growth through continuous learning. Regardless of your trading horizon, staying informed about market trends, emerging technologies, and evolving strategies is essential. Discover the significance of ongoing education in adapting to market dynamics, refining your approach, and making informed decisions throughout your trading journey.

As we explore these common strategies, understand how they serve as the bedrock of successful trading practices across varying timeframes. Whether you are engaged in short-term trades, managing medium-term positions, or adopting a long-term investment approach, integrating risk management, diversification, and continuous learning into your strategy enhances your ability to navigate the complexities of the financial markets.

"Trade Phenomena: The Path to Self-Reliance" empowers you with the knowledge and insights needed to build a resilient and adaptable trading strategy that stands the test of time. By mastering these common strategies, you equip yourself with the tools to navigate the ever-changing landscape of financial markets and foster self-reliance in your trading endeavors.

1. Risk Management:

Risk Management in Trading and Investing: A Comprehensive Guide

Risk management is a fundamental aspect of trading and investing, encompassing strategies and techniques to identify, assess, and mitigate potential losses. Effective risk management is crucial for preserving capital, achieving longterm success, and navigating the inherent uncertainties of financial markets. Here's a comprehensive guide to risk management:

Key Components of Risk Management:

1. Risk Tolerance:

Definition: The level of risk an investor or trader is willing to accept. It is influenced by factors such as financial goals, time horizon, and individual risk appetite.

Practical Application: Assessing risk tolerance helps determine the appropriate level of exposure to different asset classes and informs position sizing decisions.

2. StopLoss Orders:

Definition: Predefined orders that automatically exit a trade at a specified price to limit potential losses.

Practical Application: Setting stoploss orders helps enforce discipline and ensures that losses are kept within predetermined levels.

3. Diversification:

Definition: Spreading investments across different asset classes, industries, or geographic regions to reduce exposure to the poor performance of any single investment.

Practical Application: Diversification helps mitigate the impact of specific market or sector risks and provides a more balanced portfolio.

4. Position Sizing:

Definition: Determining the amount of capital to allocate to a specific trade, taking into account risk tolerance and stoploss levels.

Practical Application: Proper position sizing ensures that no single trade significantly impacts the overall portfolio and aligns with the investor's risk tolerance.

5. RiskReward Ratio:

Definition: The ratio of potential reward to potential risk in a trade. It helps assess whether a trade is worth taking based on the potential return compared to the risk.

Practical Application: Traders often seek trades with a favorable riskreward ratio (e.g., 2:1 or higher) to ensure that potential gains justify the risk taken.

6. Hedging:

Definition: Using financial instruments or strategies to offset the risk of adverse price movements in an asset.

Practical Application: Hedging can protect against downside risk and minimize potential losses in certain market conditions.

Risk Management Strategies:

1. Fixed Percentage Risk Model:

Description: Allocating a fixed percentage of capital to each trade, regardless of the trade's perceived risk level.

Application: This strategy helps maintain consistent risk exposure and prevents overcommitting to highrisk trades.

2. VolatilityBased Position Sizing:

Description: Adjusting position sizes based on the historical volatility of the asset.

Application: Higher volatility may warrant smaller position sizes to account for larger price swings.

3. Monte Carlo Simulation:

Description: Using statistical models to simulate various market scenarios and assess the impact on the portfolio.

Application: Monte Carlo simulations provide a forwardlooking analysis of potential portfolio performance under different market conditions.

4. Scenario Analysis:

Description: Evaluating the impact of various hypothetical scenarios on the portfolio.

Application: Traders and investors can assess how different market events may affect their positions and make informed decisions accordingly.

Practical Tips for Effective Risk Management:

1. Regular Portfolio Review:

Regularly assess and review the portfolio to ensure that it aligns with current market conditions and the investor's financial goals.

2. Adaptability:

Be adaptable and willing to adjust risk management strategies based on changes in market dynamics, economic conditions, or personal circumstances.

3. Education and Continuous Learning:

Stay informed about market trends, risk management techniques, and new developments in the financial markets. Continuous learning enhances decisionmaking capabilities.

4. Psychological Discipline:

Cultivate psychological discipline to avoid emotional decisionmaking during market fluctuations. Stick to predefined risk management strategies.

Common Mistakes to Avoid:

1. Neglecting Risk Management:

Failing to implement a robust risk management strategy exposes investors to significant losses and jeopardizes longterm financial goals.

2. Overleveraging:

Excessive use of leverage increases the potential for significant losses. Avoid overleveraging positions, especially in volatile markets.

3. Ignoring Diversification:

Concentrating investments in a single asset or sector increases vulnerability to specific risks. Diversification is a key element of effective risk management.

Risk management is a cornerstone of successful trading and investing. By employing a combination of strategies, including setting stoploss orders, diversifying portfolios, and carefully sizing positions, market participants can navigate uncertainties and position themselves for longterm success. A disciplined and proactive approach to risk management is essential for achieving financial objectives while minimizing potential losses.

Risk Management in Investment: Dos and Don'ts

Risk management is a critical aspect of successful investing, helping investors protect their capital and achieve longterm financial goals. Here are dos and don'ts to consider when implementing risk management strategies:

Dos:

1. Diversify Your Portfolio:

Do: Diversification involves spreading your investments across different asset classes, industries, and geographic regions. This helps mitigate the impact of poor performance in any single investment on your overall portfolio.

2. Set Realistic Financial Goals:

Do: Clearly define your financial goals and set realistic expectations. This will guide your investment decisions and help you assess the level of risk you're willing to take to achieve those goals.

3. Understand Your Risk Tolerance:

Do: Assess your risk tolerance based on your financial situation, investment goals, and emotional temperament. Knowing how much risk you can comfortably handle is crucial for making appropriate investment choices.

4. Use StopLoss Orders:

Do: Implement stoploss orders to automatically sell a security when its price falls to a predetermined level. This helps limit potential losses and enforces discipline in sticking to your risk management plan.

5. Stay Informed:

Do: Stay informed about economic indicators, market trends, and news that may impact your investments. Being aware of external factors allows you to make informed decisions and adjust your strategy accordingly.

6. Regularly Review Your Portfolio:

Do: Periodically review your portfolio to ensure it aligns with your goals and risk tolerance. Rebalance your portfolio if necessary, and consider adjusting your risk exposure based on changing market conditions.

7. Invest in Liquid Assets:

Do: Preferably invest in liquid assets that can be easily bought or sold without significantly impacting their market price. This provides flexibility and ensures you can exit positions when needed.

Don'ts:

1. Overlook Diversification:

Don't: Rely heavily on a single investment or asset class. Overlooking diversification exposes you to concentrated risks that can have a significant impact on your portfolio.

2. Ignore Your Risk Tolerance:

Don't: Invest in assets that exceed your risk tolerance. Ignoring your risk tolerance may lead to emotional decisionmaking during market fluctuations, potentially resulting in poor investment choices.

3. Chase High Returns Without Assessing Risks:

Don't: Pursue high returns without adequately assessing the associated risks. Highreturn opportunities often come with elevated levels of risk, and it's essential to strike a balance that aligns with your risk appetite.

4. Make Impulsive Decisions:

Don't: Make impulsive decisions based on shortterm market movements or noise. Stick to your predetermined investment plan and avoid reacting emotionally to market fluctuations.

5. Neglect Regular Portfolio Reviews:

Don't: Neglect to regularly review your portfolio. Failing to reassess and adjust your investments in response to changes in your financial situation or market conditions can expose you to unnecessary risks.

6. Ignore Liquidity Needs:

Don't: Overlook the importance of liquidity. Investing in illiquid assets without considering your potential need for cash can lead to difficulties in accessing funds when required.

7. Rely Solely on Past Performance:

Don't: Base investment decisions solely on past performance. Historical returns do not guarantee future results, and markets can change. Conduct thorough research and consider a variety of factors when making investment decisions.

Implementing effective risk management strategies requires a thoughtful and disciplined approach. By diversifying your portfolio, setting realistic goals, understanding your risk tolerance, and staying informed, you can enhance your ability to navigate the complexities of the financial markets while safeguarding your investments.

2. Diversification:

Diversification in Investment: A Comprehensive Guide

Objective:

Diversification is an investment strategy that involves spreading your capital across different asset classes, industries, and geographic regions to reduce risk and enhance the potential for longterm returns. The goal is to create a wellbalanced portfolio that can weather market fluctuations and minimize the impact of poor performance in any single investment.

Key Principles of Diversification:

1. Asset Class Diversification:

Diversify across different asset classes such as stocks, bonds, real estate, and cash equivalents. Each asset class reacts differently to economic and market conditions, providing a level of balance in the portfolio.

2. Industry and Sector Diversification:

Spread investments across various industries and sectors. Different sectors may perform differently under different economic circumstances, and diversification reduces exposure to industryspecific risks.

3. Geographic Diversification:

Invest in assets from different geographic regions to reduce exposure to countryspecific risks. Economic conditions, regulatory environments, and geopolitical factors can vary by region, impacting investment returns.

4. Company Size Diversification:

Diversify holdings across companies of different sizes. Consider including largecap, midcap, and smallcap stocks to balance exposure to companies with different market capitalizations.

5. Time Horizon Consideration:

Diversify based on your investment time horizon. For longterm goals, you might include a mix of growthoriented and incomegenerating assets. For shortterm goals, focus on more stable and liquid investments.

Benefits of Diversification:

1. Risk Reduction:

Diversification helps reduce the impact of poor performance in any single investment on the overall portfolio. While some investments may experience losses, others may perform well, balancing out the overall risk.

2. Stability and Consistency:

A diversified portfolio is more likely to provide stability and consistent returns over the long term. It can withstand market volatility and economic fluctuations better than a concentrated or undiversified portfolio.

3. Enhanced RiskReturn Profile:

By spreading investments across different assets, diversification aims to achieve an optimal balance between risk and return. It allows investors to pursue returns while managing the potential downsides.

4. Adaptability to Changing Market Conditions:

Diversification provides adaptability to changing market conditions. When certain sectors or asset classes underperform, others may outperform, helping the portfolio navigate through various market cycles.

Common Mistakes to Avoid:

1. Overconcentration in a Single Asset:

Avoid overconcentration in a single stock or asset class. Relying heavily on a particular investment increases the portfolio's vulnerability to the performance of that individual asset.

2. Ignoring Correlations:

Consider correlations between different assets. While diversification aims to spread risk, assets with high positive correlations may move in tandem during market downturns. Understanding correlations enhances the effectiveness of diversification.

3. Neglecting Regular Portfolio Reviews:

Neglecting to regularly review and rebalance your portfolio can lead to unintentional concentration in certain assets. Market movements may alter the original diversification strategy, requiring adjustments over time.

4. Failing to Consider External Factors:

External factors such as economic conditions, interest rates, and geopolitical events can impact the performance of different assets. Failing to consider these factors may result in incomplete diversification.

Implementation Tips:

1. Conduct Thorough Research:

Conduct thorough research when selecting assets for your portfolio. Understand the characteristics and risks associated with each investment to make informed decisions.

2. Regularly Review and Rebalance:

Regularly review your portfolio and rebalance as needed. Market movements may cause shifts in the original asset allocation, and periodic adjustments ensure that your portfolio remains diversified.

3. Consider Professional Advice:

Seek advice from financial professionals who can help design a diversified portfolio based on your financial goals, risk tolerance, and investment horizon.

4. Stay Informed:

Stay informed about market trends, economic indicators, and global events. Being aware of changing conditions allows you to make proactive decisions to maintain effective diversification.

Diversification is a fundamental principle of risk management in investing. By carefully constructing a diversified portfolio that considers various asset classes, sectors, and geographic regions, investors can potentially achieve a more balanced and resilient investment strategy over the long term.

3. Continuous Learning:

Continuous Learning for Growth

Continuous learning, also known as lifelong learning, is the ongoing, voluntary, and selfmotivated pursuit of knowledge and personal development. In today's rapidly changing world, embracing a mindset of continuous learning is crucial for personal growth, career advancement, and staying relevant in various domains. Here are key reasons why continuous learning is important:

1. Adaptability to Change:

In the Professional Sphere: Continuous learning allows individuals to adapt to changes in their industries. New technologies, methodologies, and market trends emerge regularly, and those who stay updated remain valuable assets to their employers.

In Personal Growth: Life itself is dynamic, and learning helps individuals adapt to personal changes, whether it's acquiring new life skills, managing relationships, or navigating life transitions.

2. Career Advancement:

Professional Development: Continuous learning enhances skills and knowledge, making individuals more competitive in the job market. It opens up opportunities for promotions, career switches, and increased responsibilities.

Entrepreneurial Endeavors: For entrepreneurs, staying informed about industry trends, market dynamics, and innovative practices is essential for the success and sustainability of their ventures.

3. Skill Enhancement:

Skill Relevance: Continuous learning ensures that skills remain relevant in a rapidly evolving job market. This is particularly crucial in industries driven by technology, where skill obsolescence is a real concern.

Acquiring New Skills: Learning provides an avenue for acquiring new skills, whether they are directly related to one's profession or hobbies. Developing a diverse skill set increases personal effectiveness and versatility.

4. Cognitive Benefits:

Mental Agility: Engaging in continuous learning exercises the brain, promoting mental agility and cognitive flexibility. Learning new things enhances problemsolving abilities and critical thinking skills.

Memory Enhancement: Lifelong learning has been linked to improved memory and cognitive function, contributing to overall mental wellbeing.

5. Personal Fulfillment:

Pursuing Passions: Learning allows individuals to explore their interests and passions. Whether it's learning a musical instrument, a new language, or delving into a hobby, continuous learning adds depth and fulfillment to life.

SelfDiscovery: Continuous learning can contribute to selfdiscovery and personal growth. It provides opportunities for individuals to better understand themselves, their values, and what brings them joy and satisfaction.

6. Networking and Collaboration:

Professional Networking: Learning often involves connecting with others who share similar interests. Building a network of individuals with diverse knowledge and skills can lead to collaborative opportunities and idea exchange.

Community Engagement: Continuous learning can extend beyond

personal and professional realms into community engagement. Participating in educational or cultural activities fosters connections and a sense of belonging.

7. FutureProofing:

Anticipating Trends: Continuous learners are better positioned to anticipate industry trends and emerging opportunities. This proactive approach helps individuals and organizations stay ahead in a competitive landscape.

Adopting Future Technologies: In the digital age, staying abreast of technological advancements is essential. Continuous learners are more likely to embrace and adapt to new technologies, ensuring they remain relevant in a techdriven world.

Tips for Cultivating a Culture of Continuous Learning:

1. Set Learning Goals:

Define clear learning goals, both shortterm and longterm. These goals can be related to professional development, personal interests, or skill acquisition.

2. Utilize Online Resources:

Take advantage of online platforms, courses, and educational resources. The internet provides a wealth of information, from formal courses on platforms like Coursera and edX to informal tutorials and webinars.

3. Read Regularly:

Read books, articles, and research papers to stay informed about your industry, current affairs, and areas of personal interest. Reading enhances knowledge and critical thinking.

4. Attend Workshops and Conferences:

Participate in workshops, conferences, and seminars related to your field. These events provide opportunities for networking and exposure to the latest industry trends.

5. Embrace a Growth Mindset:

Adopt a growth mindset, which involves seeing challenges as opportunities for growth. Embrace the idea that abilities can be developed through dedication and hard work.

6. Seek Feedback:

Seek constructive feedback on your learning journey. Whether it's from mentors, colleagues, or online communities, feedback can provide valuable insights and guide your learning path.

7. Encourage a Learning Environment:

Foster a culture of continuous learning within your workplace or community. Encourage knowledgesharing, mentorship, and the recognition of learning achievements.

8. Experiment and Apply Knowledge:

Apply what you learn through practical experiments and realworld applications. This reinforces understanding and helps transfer knowledge into practical skills.

Trading Strategies: Dos and Don'ts for Success

Trading in financial markets requires a strategic approach to navigate the complexities and uncertainties. Here are key dos and don'ts to enhance your trading strategies:

Dos:

1. Do Develop a Trading Plan:

Why: A well-defined trading plan outlines your goals, risk tolerance, entry and exit criteria, and overall strategy.

How: Clearly define your objectives, preferred asset classes, risk management rules, and performance metrics.

2. Do Practice Risk Management:

Why: Protecting your capital is paramount. Implementing risk management rules helps prevent substantial losses.

How: Set stop-loss orders, diversify your portfolio, and determine position sizes based on your risk tolerance.

3. Do Stay Informed:

Why: Markets are dynamic and influenced by various factors. Staying informed is crucial for making informed trading decisions.

How: Regularly follow financial news, monitor economic indicators, and stay updated on relevant developments in your chosen markets.

4. Do Diversify Your Portfolio:

Why: Diversification helps spread risk and reduce the impact of poor performance in a single asset or sector.

How: Invest in different asset classes, industries, and geographic regions to create a well-balanced portfolio.

5. Do Set Realistic Goals:

Why: Establishing achievable and realistic goals helps you stay focused and motivated.

How: Define both short-term and long-term goals based on your financial objectives and risk tolerance.

6. Do Utilize Technical and Fundamental Analysis:

Why: Combining technical analysis with fundamental analysis provides a comprehensive view of market conditions.

How: Use technical indicators, chart patterns, and also consider fundamental factors such as economic data and corporate performance.

7. Do Keep Emotions in Check:

Why: Emotional decision-making can lead to impulsive actions and poor choices.

How: Stick to your trading plan, avoid chasing losses, and remain disciplined during both winning and losing streaks.

8. Do Continuously Learn and Adapt:

Why: Markets evolve, and continuous learning is essential for staying ahead.

How: Read books, attend webinars, follow market analysts, and adapt your strategies based on changing market conditions.

Don'ts:

1. Don't Trade Without a Plan:

Why: Trading without a plan is akin to navigating without a map, leading to aimless and risky decisions.

How: Develop a comprehensive trading plan that guides your actions and aligns with your financial goals.

2. Don't Ignore Risk Management:

Why: Neglecting risk management increases the likelihood of significant losses.

How: Always use stop-loss orders, diversify your investments, and avoid overleveraging.

3. Don't Chase Losses:

Why: Attempting to recover losses through impulsive trading can lead to further setbacks.

How: Stick to your plan, accept losses as part of trading, and avoid making emotional decisions based on recent losses.

4. Don't Rely Solely on Hunches:

Why: Trading based on gut feelings without proper analysis is speculative and risky.

How: Base your decisions on a combination of technical and fundamental analysis rather than intuition alone.

5. Don't Overtrade:

Why: Excessive trading can lead to increased transaction costs and potential mistakes.

How: Stick to your predefined trading plan, avoid unnecessary transactions, and prioritize quality over quantity.

6. Don't Follow the Herd Blindly:

Why: Blindly following the crowd can lead to herd mentality and poor decision-making.

How: Conduct your own analysis, be aware of market sentiment, and make independent decisions.

7. Don't Neglect Continuous Learning:

Why: Failing to adapt to changing market conditions can result in outdated strategies.

How: Stay informed, read market analyses, and actively seek opportunities for continuous learning.

8. Don't Trade Without Understanding:

Why: Trading complex financial instruments without understanding the underlying mechanics can lead to significant losses.

How: Ensure you have a solid understanding of the markets, instruments, and strategies you are employing.

Remember that successful trading is a continuous learning process. By adhering to these dos and don'ts, you can build a robust foundation for effective and disciplined trading strategies.

Benefits of Trading Strategies

Trading strategies offer various benefits to traders and investors, helping them navigate the complex and dynamic nature of financial markets. Here are key advantages associated with using trading strategies:

1. Objective Decision-Making:

Benefits: Trading strategies provide a systematic and objective framework for decision-making. They help traders avoid impulsive and emotional reactions to market fluctuations.

How: Strategies are based on predefined rules and criteria, ensuring that trading decisions are made in a disciplined manner.

2. Risk Management:

Benefits: Trading strategies incorporate risk management principles, allowing traders to control and mitigate potential losses.

How: Strategies often include setting stop-loss orders, determining position sizes based on risk tolerance, and diversifying portfolios to spread risk.

3. Consistency:

Benefits: Trading strategies promote consistency in trading activities. Consistent application of a well-defined strategy helps maintain a steady approach over time.

How: Traders adhere to predetermined rules, entry and exit criteria, and risk management practices, reducing the impact of emotional decision-making.

4. Improved Timing:

Benefits: Strategies help traders identify optimal entry and exit points, improving the timing of trades.

How: Technical indicators, chart patterns, and other tools incorporated into strategies assist in identifying potential trend reversals, breakouts, or other market conditions.

5. Reduced Emotional Stress:

Benefits: Having a trading strategy reduces emotional stress and anxiety associated with decision-making during market fluctuations.

How: By relying on predefined rules and criteria, traders avoid impulsive reactions to market news or short-term price movements.

6. Efficient Use of Time:

Benefits: Trading strategies streamline the decision-making process, making trading more efficient.

How: Traders can focus on executing the strategy rather than constantly analyzing market conditions, saving time and effort.

7. Quantifiable Performance Metrics:

Benefits: Strategies provide quantifiable metrics to assess performance, allowing traders to evaluate the effectiveness of their approach.

How: Performance metrics may include win-loss ratios, risk-reward ratios, and other key indicators that help measure the success of the strategy.

8. Adaptability:

Benefits: Trading strategies can be adapted to different market conditions and timeframes.

How: Traders can modify or develop new strategies based on evolving market dynamics, ensuring relevance and effectiveness in various scenarios.

9. Education and Learning:

Benefits: Following a trading strategy promotes continuous learning and improvement.

How: Traders gain insights into market dynamics, technical analysis, and fundamental factors through the implementation and evaluation of strategies.

10. Goal Alignment:

Benefits: Strategies align with traders' financial goals, providing a structured approach to achieving specific objectives.

How: Traders can tailor their strategies to match their risk tolerance, investment horizon, and desired outcomes.

11. Backtesting and Optimization:

Benefits: Strategies can be backtested using historical data, allowing traders to assess how the strategy would have performed in past market conditions.

How: By analyzing historical data, traders can identify strengths and weaknesses in the strategy, leading to optimization and refinement.

12. Flexibility:

Benefits: Strategies can be adapted to different trading styles and preferences.

How: Traders can choose or develop strategies that align with their preferred timeframes, risk appetite, and market focus (e.g., day trading, swing trading, long-term investing).

13. Increased Confidence:

Benefits: Trading with a well-defined strategy boosts traders' confidence in their decision-making.

How: Knowing that trades are based on a systematic approach provides a sense of confidence, reducing second-guessing and hesitations.

14. Enhanced Accountability:

Benefits: Trading strategies create accountability by establishing clear rules for actions and outcomes.

How: Traders can evaluate their performance against the predefined rules of the strategy, enhancing accountability for their actions.

15. Adherence to Market Trends:

Benefits: Strategies help traders identify and align with prevailing market trends.

How: By incorporating trend-following indicators and analysis, traders can capitalize on market trends rather than going against them.

In summary, trading strategies offer a structured and disciplined approach to trading, providing numerous benefits such as risk management, consistent decision-making, and adaptability to changing market conditions. Traders can leverage these advantages to enhance their overall trading performance and achieve their financial goals.

Risks of Trading Strategies

While trading strategies offer numerous benefits, it's essential to be aware of the potential risks and challenges associated with their implementation. Here are some key risks associated with trading strategies:

1. Market Risks:

Description: Unforeseen market events, volatility, or sudden price movements can impact the effectiveness of a trading strategy.

Mitigation: Implement risk management measures such as setting stop-loss orders and being aware of major economic events.

2. Over-Optimization:

Description: Excessive optimization of a strategy based on historical data may result in overfitting, where the strategy performs well on past data but poorly on new, unseen data.

Mitigation: Use out-of-sample testing, avoid excessive parameter tweaking, and ensure the strategy has a robust foundation.

3. Changing Market Conditions:

Description: Market conditions can change, rendering a previously successful strategy less effective.

Mitigation: Regularly review and adapt strategies to evolving market dynamics. Be prepared to modify or switch strategies when necessary.

4. Lack of Flexibility:

Description: A strategy that is too rigid may fail to adapt to changing market conditions or unexpected events.

Mitigation: Build flexibility into the strategy, allowing for adjustments based on new information or shifts in market sentiment.

5. Execution Risks:

Description: Issues related to order execution, slippage, and liquidity can impact the actual performance of a strategy.

Mitigation: Choose reputable brokers, consider the liquidity of the assets being traded, and be aware of potential slippage.

6. Data Quality and Availability:

Description: Poor-quality or insufficient historical data can lead to inaccurate backtesting results, affecting the reliability of a strategy.

Mitigation: Use high-quality data for backtesting, and be cautious about the limitations of historical data in predicting future performance.

7. Psychological Factors:

Description: Traders may deviate from the strategy due to emotions such as fear, greed, or impatience.

Mitigation: Cultivate emotional discipline, adhere to the predefined rules of the strategy, and avoid making impulsive decisions.

8. Model Assumptions:

Description: Trading strategies are often based on certain assumptions about market behavior that may not always hold true.

Mitigation: Regularly review and validate the assumptions underlying the strategy. Be aware of changing market dynamics that may invalidate assumptions.

9. Black Swan Events:

Description: Rare and extreme events, often unforeseeable, can have a significant impact on financial markets.

Mitigation: Diversify portfolios, use risk management tools, and be prepared for the possibility of unexpected market events.

10. Technology Risks:

Description: Technical issues such as system failures, connectivity problems, or data inaccuracies can disrupt the execution of a strategy.

Mitigation: Use reliable technology infrastructure, implement backup systems, and stay informed about potential technical risks.

11. Regulatory Changes:

Description: Changes in regulatory environments, tax laws, or market rules can affect the viability of certain trading strategies.

Mitigation: Stay informed about regulatory developments and be prepared to adapt strategies accordingly.

12. Strategy Decay:

Description: As more market participants adopt a particular strategy, its effectiveness may diminish over time.

Mitigation: Continuously monitor the performance of the strategy and be prepared to adjust or switch to a new approach if needed.

13. Unexpected News Events:

Description: News events, especially unexpected ones, can lead to rapid market movements that may not align with the strategy's assumptions.

Mitigation: Stay informed about economic calendars, news releases, and geopolitical events that may impact the markets.

14. Lack of Real-Time Adaptation:

Description: Strategies that rely on historical data may not adapt quickly enough to rapidly changing market conditions.

Mitigation: Incorporate real-time data feeds and consider strategies that can dynamically adjust to changing market dynamics.

15. Liquidity Risks:

Description: Limited liquidity in certain markets or assets may result in difficulty executing trades at desired prices.

Mitigation: Consider liquidity factors when selecting assets to trade, and be aware of potential liquidity risks.

Trading strategies come with inherent risks, and traders should approach them with a clear understanding of potential challenges. Regular monitoring, adaptability, and a commitment to risk management are crucial for navigating the uncertainties of financial markets successfully. It's also important to acknowledge that no strategy can guarantee profits, and past performance is not always indicative of future results.

CHAPTER 2

TECHNICAL ANALYSIS TECHNIQUES

In the second chapter of "Trade Phenomena: The Path to Self-Reliance," we dive into the intricate world of technical analysis, a cornerstone of successful trading strategies. This chapter is designed to equip traders, both novice and experienced, with a comprehensive understanding of technical analysis techniques, empowering them to make informed decisions in dynamic market conditions.

Topics Covered:

❖ **Candlestick Patterns:**

Explore the art and significance of candlestick patterns, deciphering the visual language of price movements. From Doji and Hammer to Engulfing and Morning Star, unravel the patterns that provide insights into market sentiment and potential trend reversals.

❖ **Support and Resistance Levels:**

Navigate the crucial concepts of support and resistance, essential tools for identifying key price levels in the market. Understand how these levels influence decision-making, serving as a foundation for strategic entry and exit points.

❖ **Indicators (RSI, MACD, Moving Averages):**

Delve into the realm of technical indicators, including Relative Strength Index (RSI), Moving Average Convergence Divergence (MACD), and Moving Averages. Uncover their significance in gauging market momentum, trend reversals, and potential entry or exit signals.

❖ Technical Analysis Dos and Don'ts for Success:

Gain insights into the best practices and pitfalls of technical analysis. Understand the dos and don'ts that can significantly impact the effectiveness of your trading decisions.

❖ Benefits of Technical Analysis:

Explore the numerous advantages that technical analysis offers to traders. From its ability to provide clear visual representations of market trends to aiding in risk management, discover the practical benefits that enhance your trading strategy.

❖ Risks of Technical Analysis:

Acknowledge the potential risks associated with relying solely on technical analysis. While a powerful tool, understanding its limitations and the challenges it may pose is crucial for a well-rounded and resilient trading approach.

This chapter serves as a comprehensive guide, offering not only theoretical insights into technical analysis but also practical tips and strategies for implementation. Whether you are looking to refine your existing technical analysis skills or are just starting your trading journey, "Trade Phenomena" provides the knowledge and tools needed to navigate the dynamic landscape of financial markets successfully.

Candlestick Patterns:

Candlestick patterns offer insights into market sentiment. Recognizing patterns like doji, engulfing, and hammer can help predict potential price movements.

Understanding Candlestick Patterns in Technical Analysis

Candlestick patterns are visual representations of price movements in financial markets, commonly used in technical analysis to identify potential trend reversals, trend continuations, or market indecision. Each candlestick on a price chart provides information about the open, high, low, and close prices for a specific time period. Analyzing the patterns formed by these candlesticks helps traders make informed decisions about market direction and potential entry or exit points.

Key Elements of Candlestick Patterns:

1. Body:

The body of a candlestick represents the price range between the open and close for a specific time period. A filled (or bearish) candle has a lower close than open, while a hollow (or bullish) candle has a higher close than open.

2. Wicks or Shadows:

The wicks or shadows extend from the top and bottom of the candle body, indicating the highest and lowest prices reached during the time period. The upper wick extends from the top of the body to the high price, and the lower wick extends from the bottom of the body to the low price.

Common Candlestick Patterns:

1. Doji:

A Doji has a small body, indicating that the open and close prices are very close or identical. It suggests market indecision and can signal a potential reversal.

2. Hammer:

A Hammer has a small body with a long lower wick and little to no upper wick. It indicates a potential bullish reversal after a downtrend.

3. Shooting Star:

The Shooting Star has a small body with a long upper wick and little to no lower wick. It signals a potential bearish reversal after an uptrend.

4. Engulfing Patterns:

Bullish Engulfing: A bullish candle fully engulfs the previous bearish candle, suggesting a potential reversal to the upside.

Bearish Engulfing: A bearish candle fully engulfs the previous bullish candle, indicating a potential reversal to the downside.

5. Morning Star and Evening Star:

Morning Star: Consists of a bearish candle, followed by a Doji or smallbodied candle, and then a bullish candle. It signals a potential bullish reversal.

Evening Star: Comprises a bullish candle, followed by a Doji or smallbodied candle, and then a bearish candle. It indicates a potential bearish reversal.

6. Harami Patterns:

Bullish Harami: A small bullish candle is engulfed by a larger bearish candle, signaling a potential bearish reversal.

Bearish Harami: A small bearish candle is engulfed by a larger bullish candle, suggesting a potential bullish reversal.

Implementation Tips:

1. Confirmation with Other Indicators:

Confirm candlestick patterns with other technical indicators, such as moving averages, trendlines, or oscillators, to increase the reliability of signals.

2. Consider Timeframes:

Analyze candlestick patterns in the context of different timeframes. Patterns on longer timeframes may carry more significance than those on shorter timeframes.

3. Combine Multiple Patterns:

Combine multiple candlestick patterns or use them in conjunction with other chart patterns to strengthen your analysis.

4. Understand Market Context:

Consider the overall market context, including trends and support/resistance levels, when interpreting candlestick patterns. Context provides a more comprehensive view of potential price movements.

5. Practice and Experience:

Gain experience and practice recognizing candlestick patterns on historical charts. This helps develop a better understanding of their significance in various market conditions.

Common Mistakes to Avoid:

1. Overreliance on Patterns:

Avoid relying solely on candlestick patterns for trading decisions. Consider them as part of a broader analysis that includes other technical and fundamental factors.

2. Ignoring Market Context:

Don't ignore the broader market context. Understand the prevailing trend, key support/resistance levels, and overall market conditions when interpreting candlestick patterns.

3. Failure to Confirm:

Avoid making decisions based solely on a single candlestick pattern. Look for confirmation from other indicators or price action to enhance the reliability of signals.

4. Ignoring Risk Management:

Incorporate risk management principles into your trading strategy. Set stoploss orders and determine your risk tolerance before entering trades based on candlestick patterns.

Dos and Don'ts for Effective Trading

Candlestick patterns are powerful tools in technical analysis, providing insights into market sentiment and potential price movements. However, using them effectively requires a combination of knowledge, experience, and discipline. Here are some dos and don'ts for trading with candlestick patterns:

Dos:

1. Learn and Understand Candlestick Patterns:

Do: Invest time in learning and understanding various candlestick patterns. Recognize the significance of individual patterns and their potential implications for price movements.

2. Combine with Other Technical Analysis Tools:

Do: Use candlestick patterns in conjunction with other technical analysis tools, such as trendlines, support and resistance levels, and indicators like RSI or MACD. This helps validate signals and enhance the overall analysis.

3. Consider the Overall Market Context:

Do: Analyze candlestick patterns within the broader market context. Consider the prevailing trend, key support/resistance levels, and recent news or events that may impact the market.

4. Use Confirmation Signals:

Do: Look for confirmation signals before acting on a candlestick pattern. These can include additional candlestick patterns, volume analysis, or confirmation from other technical indicators.

5. Practice Risk Management:

Do: Implement proper risk management strategies. Set stoploss orders to limit potential losses and adhere to a consistent riskreward ratio.

6. Adapt to Different Timeframes:

Do: Consider the timeframe of your trading. Some candlestick patterns may have more significance on longer timeframes, while others are relevant in shorterterm trading.

Don'ts:

1. Rely Solely on Candlestick Patterns:

Don't: Depend solely on candlestick patterns for trading decisions. Consider them as part of a comprehensive analysis that includes other technical and fundamental factors.

2. Overlook the Market Context:

Don't: Ignore the overall market context. A candlestick pattern may have different implications in different market conditions, and understanding the broader picture is crucial.

3. Chase Patterns:

Don't: Chase after candlestick patterns. Wait for confirmation and ensure that the pattern aligns with the overall analysis and your trading strategy before entering a trade.

4. Disregard Risk Management:

Don't: Neglect risk management principles. Even with a seemingly strong candlestick pattern, it's essential to manage risk and avoid exposing yourself to significant losses.

5. Ignore News and Events:

Don't: Disregard news and events that may impact the market. Sudden developments can override the signals provided by candlestick patterns.

6. Become Overconfident:

Don't: Become overconfident based solely on the recognition of candlestick patterns. Maintain a humble approach and continuously reassess your trading strategy.

Candlestick patterns can be valuable tools for traders, but they should be used judiciously and as part of a broader trading strategy. By combining them with other technical analysis tools, considering the overall market context, and practicing disciplined risk management, traders can enhance their ability to make informed and effective decisions in the dynamic world of financial markets.

Support and Resistance Levels:

Identifying key support and resistance levels is crucial for understanding where prices might reverse or consolidate.

Support and Resistance in Technical Analysis

Support and resistance levels are key concepts in technical analysis, providing valuable insights into potential price movements in financial markets. Traders and investors use these levels to make informed decisions about entry and exit points, as well as to gauge the strength of trends. Let's explore the definitions, characteristics, and practical applications of support and resistance.

Support Level:

Definition: A support level is a price level at which a financial asset, such as a stock or currency pair, historically experiences a high demand, preventing the price from falling further. It acts as a floor for the price, as buyers are inclined to enter the market and prevent further declines.

Characteristics:

1. Historical Significance: Support levels are identified based on historical price movements. These levels often coincide with areas where the price has bounced back or reversed in the past.

2. Buying Interest: Support levels are associated with increased buying interest. Traders and investors see the asset as attractively priced at these levels, leading to a surge in buying activity.

3. Psychological Impact: Certain round numbers or significant price levels may act as psychological support. For example, prices ending in 50 or 100 may attract buying interest.

Practical Application:

Traders often look for buying opportunities when an asset approaches a support level. If the price reaches a historical support level and shows signs of a potential reversal, it may present an attractive entry point.

Support levels can be used to set stoploss orders. If a trader enters a long position at a support level, a stoploss order may be placed just below the support level to limit potential losses if the price breaks through.

Resistance Level:

Definition: A resistance level is a price level at which a financial asset historically encounters selling interest, preventing the price from rising further. It acts as a ceiling for the price, as sellers are motivated to enter the market and resist further upward movements.

Characteristics:

1. Historical Significance: Resistance levels are identified based on historical price movements. These levels often coincide with areas where the price has faced selling pressure or reversed in the past.

2. Selling Interest: Resistance levels are associated with increased selling interest. Traders and investors see the asset as relatively overvalued at these levels, leading to a surge in selling activity.

3. Psychological Impact: Round numbers or significant price levels can act as psychological resistance. Prices ending in 00 or 50 may attract selling interest.

Practical Application:

Traders often look for selling opportunities when an asset approaches a resistance level. If the price reaches a historical resistance level and shows signs of a potential reversal, it may present an attractive point to exit a long position or enter a short position.

Resistance levels can be used to set profittaking targets. If a trader enters a short position at a resistance level, a takeprofit order may be placed just above the resistance level to secure gains if the price reverses.

Common Mistakes to Avoid:

1. *Ignoring Historical Data:* Failing to consider historical price movements when identifying support and resistance levels can lead to inaccurate assessments.

2. *Overemphasizing Single Levels:* Relying solely on a single support or resistance level without considering the broader context can result in missed opportunities or increased risk.

3. *Not Adapting to Changing Conditions:* Support and resistance levels may shift over time. Failing to adapt to changing market conditions can lead to outdated analysis.

Dos and Don'ts for Effective Trading

Support and resistance levels are foundational concepts in technical analysis, offering valuable insights into potential price movements. To use them effectively, traders should follow certain dos and don'ts to enhance their decisionmaking process:

Dos:

1. Identify Clear Support and Resistance Zones:

Do: Identify clear and welldefined support and resistance zones on price charts. Look for areas where the price has historically bounced off or struggled to move beyond.

2. Use Multiple Timeframes:

Do: Analyze support and resistance levels across multiple timeframes. What may appear as a significant level on a shorter timeframe might have a different significance on a longer one.

3. Combine with Other Technical Analysis Tools:

Do: Use support and resistance levels in conjunction with other technical analysis tools, such as trendlines, moving averages, and indicators. This helps validate signals and provides a more comprehensive analysis.

4. Recognize Dynamic and Static Levels:

Do: Distinguish between dynamic (changing) and static (fixed) support/resistance levels. Dynamic levels may include moving averages, while static levels are based on horizontal price levels.

5. Consider Psychological Levels:

Do: Take into account psychological levels, such as round numbers or significant price levels ending in 00 or 50. These levels often attract attention from traders and can act as support or resistance.

6. Wait for Confirmation:

Do: Wait for confirmation before making trading decisions based on support or resistance. Look for additional technical signals, candlestick patterns, or other forms of confirmation.

Don'ts:

1. Assume Support or Resistance Holds Indefinitely:

Don't: Assume that a support or resistance level will hold indefinitely. Market conditions can change, and levels may be breached under certain circumstances.

2. Neglect Market Context:

Don't: Neglect the overall market context. Consider the prevailing trend, recent news, or economic events that may impact the significance of support and resistance levels.

3. Overcrowd Your Chart:

Don't: Overcrowd your chart with too many support and resistance lines. Keep it clean and focus on the most relevant and significant levels.

4. Disregard Price Action:

Don't: Disregard price action when approaching support or resistance. Observe how the price reacts around these levels and look for confirmation through price behavior.

5. Ignore Multiple Touches:

Don't: Ignore the importance of multiple touches at a support or resistance level. The more times a level has been tested and held, the more significant it may become.

6. Rely Solely on Historical Levels:

Don't: Rely solely on historical support and resistance levels. Market dynamics change, and it's essential to adapt to current conditions rather than relying solely on past data.

Effectively utilizing support and resistance levels requires a balanced approach that considers both historical price data and current market conditions. By following these dos and don'ts, traders can enhance their ability to identify key levels, make informed decisions, and navigate the dynamic landscape of financial markets.

Indicators (RSI, MACD, Moving Averages):

Technical indicators such as the Relative Strength Index (RSI), Moving Average Convergence Divergence (MACD), and various moving averages help traders analyze market conditions and trends.

Decoding Technical Indicators: RSI, MACD, Moving Averages

Technical indicators are essential tools in analyzing financial markets, providing insights into price trends, momentum, and potential reversal points. Here, we'll explore three widely used indicators: Relative Strength Index (RSI), Moving Average Convergence Divergence (MACD), and Moving Averages.

Relative Strength Index (RSI):

Definition:

The RSI is a momentum oscillator that measures the speed and change of price movements. It ranges from 0 to 100 and is typically used to identify overbought or oversold conditions in a market.

Key Characteristics:

1. Overbought and Oversold Levels: RSI values above 70 are considered overbought, suggesting a potential reversal or pullback. Values below 30 are considered oversold, indicating a potential upward reversal.

2. Divergence Signals: Divergence between RSI and price movements can signal a potential reversal. Bullish divergence occurs when RSI makes higher lows while prices make lower lows, and vice versa for bearish divergence.

Practical Application:

Overbought/Oversold Conditions: Traders may consider selling when RSI is above 70 and buying when it's below 30. However, it's important to use these signals in conjunction with other indicators and market context.

Divergence Signals: Divergence between RSI and price can be a useful early warning signal for potential trend changes.

Moving Average Convergence Divergence (MACD):

Definition:

MACD is a trendfollowing momentum indicator that shows the relationship between two moving averages of an asset's price. It consists of the MACD line, the signal line, and a histogram.

Key Characteristics:

1. MACD Line and Signal Line Crossovers: Bullish signals occur when the MACD line crosses above the signal line, suggesting potential upward momentum. Bearish signals occur when the MACD line crosses below the signal line, indicating potential downward momentum.

2. Histogram Interpretation: The histogram represents the difference between the MACD line and the signal line. Rising histograms suggest increasing momentum, while falling histograms indicate decreasing momentum.

Practical Application:

Crossovers: Traders may use MACD crossovers as signals for potential entry or exit points in the market. However, it's crucial to consider other indicators and market conditions.

Divergence: Divergence between MACD and price movements can provide insights into potential trend reversals.

Moving Averages:

Definition:

Moving averages smooth out price data to create a single flowing line, providing a clearer picture of the overall trend. The two primary types are the Simple Moving Average (SMA) and the Exponential Moving Average (EMA).

Key Characteristics:

1. Trend Identification: Moving averages help identify the direction of the prevailing trend. In an uptrend, prices are typically above the moving average, and in a downtrend, prices are below.

2. Support and Resistance: Moving averages can act as dynamic support or resistance levels. Traders may observe bounces or breakouts when prices interact with moving averages.

Practical Application:

Trend Confirmation: Traders often use moving averages to confirm the existence of a trend before making trading decisions.

Crossovers: Moving average crossovers, such as the Golden Cross (shortterm crossing above the longterm) and Death Cross (shortterm crossing below the longterm), can be used to identify potential trend changes.

Common Mistakes to Avoid:

1. Overreliance on a Single Indicator: Using a single indicator in isolation without considering other factors may lead to incomplete analysis.

2. Ignoring Market Context: Failing to consider broader market conditions, economic events, or news that may impact price movements.

3. Not Adjusting for Timeframes: Different timeframes may yield different signals. Traders should be aware of the chosen timeframe's implications on the reliability of signals.

RSI, MACD, Moving Averages: Dos and Don'ts

Indicators such as Relative Strength Index (RSI), Moving Average Convergence Divergence (MACD), and Moving Averages are popular tools in technical analysis. To use them effectively, traders should adhere to certain dos and don'ts to enhance their decisionmaking process:

Dos:

1. Understand the Basics of Each Indicator:

Do: Invest time in understanding the fundamentals of RSI, MACD, and Moving Averages. Learn how each indicator is calculated and what it signifies in terms of market trends and momentum.

2. Use Multiple Indicators for Confirmation:

Do: Use multiple indicators in combination to confirm signals. For example, if RSI suggests overbought conditions, check for confirmation from other indicators or price action.

3. Adapt Indicators to Different Timeframes:

Do: Adapt the settings of indicators to different timeframes. The parameters that work well on a daily chart may not be as effective on an hourly or shorter timeframe.

4. Combine with Price Action and Support/Resistance:

Do: Combine indicator signals with price action and support/resistance levels for a more comprehensive analysis. Confirming signals across different analysis tools increases their reliability.

5. Regularly Review and Adjust Parameters:

Do: Regularly review and adjust the parameters of your indicators based on changing market conditions. Periodically reassess the effectiveness of your chosen settings.

6. Use Moving Averages for Trend Identification:

Do: Use Moving Averages for trend identification. The crossover of shortterm and longterm moving averages can signal potential changes in the direction of the trend.

Don'ts:

1. Overcrowd Your Chart with Indicators:

Don't: Overload your chart with too many indicators. This can lead to analysis paralysis and confusion. Focus on a few key indicators that complement your trading strategy.

2. Rely Solely on Indicators:

Don't: Rely solely on indicators for trading decisions. Always consider other factors, including fundamental analysis, market sentiment, and economic events.

3. Ignore Changing Market Conditions:

Don't: Ignore changing market conditions. What works well in a trending market may not be as effective in a ranging or choppy market. Be adaptable.

4. Disregard Risk Management:

Don't: Disregard risk management principles. Even if indicators provide a strong signal, set stoploss orders and manage your risk appropriately.

5. Chase Overbought or Oversold Conditions:

Don't: Chase overbought or oversold conditions blindly. Wait for confirmation and be cautious of potential reversals.

6. Ignore Divergence Signals:

Don't: Ignore divergence signals. Divergence between an indicator and price action can signal potential trend reversals and should not be overlooked.

Effectively utilizing RSI, MACD, and Moving Averages requires a balanced and informed approach. Traders should integrate these indicators into a broader trading strategy, considering various factors and adapting to changing market conditions. By following these dos and don'ts, traders can enhance their analytical skills and make more informed decisions in the dynamic world of financial markets.

Technical Analysis Dos and Don'ts for Success

Technical analysis is a vital tool for traders seeking to make informed decisions based on historical price data and market indicators. However, like any approach, there are essential dos and don'ts, as well as benefits and risks associated with technical analysis techniques.

Do: Embrace a Holistic Approach

Combine Indicators: Utilize a combination of technical indicators, such as moving averages, Relative Strength Index (RSI), and MACD, to gain a comprehensive understanding of market conditions.

Backtesting: Test your chosen technical analysis strategies on historical data to evaluate their effectiveness before applying them to live trading.

Stay Informed: Continuously educate yourself on new technical analysis tools and refine your strategies based on the evolving market landscape.

Don't: Rely Solely on Technical Analysis

Neglect Fundamental Analysis: While technical analysis is powerful, it should not be the sole basis for trading decisions. Combine it with fundamental analysis to form a wellrounded strategy.

Overcomplicate Strategies: Avoid using too many indicators or creating overly complex strategies. Simplicity can often be more effective in technical analysis.

Ignore Market Sentiment: Technical analysis is a valuable tool, but it should be complemented by an awareness of market sentiment and external factors that may impact prices.

Benefits of Technical Analysis

Predictive Insights: Technical analysis provides traders with insights into potential future price movements based on historical data patterns.

Objective DecisionMaking: It offers a more objective approach to decisionmaking, allowing traders to make informed choices based on data rather than emotions.

Timing Entry and Exit Points: Technical analysis assists in identifying optimal entry and exit points for trades, improving the overall precision of trading strategies.

Risks of Technical Analysis

Not Foolproof: Technical analysis is not foolproof. Markets can be influenced by unforeseen events, rendering historical patterns less reliable.

Subjectivity: Interpretation of chart patterns and indicators can be subjective. Different traders may draw different conclusions from the same data.

Limited to Historical Data: Technical analysis relies on historical data, and past performance does not guarantee future results.

In conclusion, technical analysis is a powerful tool when used judiciously. By embracing a holistic approach, avoiding overreliance, and staying informed, traders can harness the benefits of technical analysis while managing its inherent risks in the dynamic cryptocurrency market.

CHAPTER 3

FUNDAMENTAL ANALYSIS

In the heart of "Trade Phenomena: The Path to Self-Reliance," Chapter "Fundamental Analysis," serves as a cornerstone for traders seeking a comprehensive understanding of the financial markets. This section delves into the core principles of fundamental analysis, providing invaluable insights and strategies to equip traders with the knowledge necessary for success.

Topics Covered:

❖ **Tokenomics:**
Explore the intricate dynamics of tokenomics, unraveling the economic principles governing cryptocurrencies. Gain a profound understanding of the factors influencing token supply, distribution, and utility within the crypto ecosystem.

❖ **News and Events:**
Navigate the ever-changing landscape of financial markets by dissecting the impact of news and events on asset prices. Learn to discern relevant information, interpret market sentiment, and make informed decisions in the face of breaking developments.

❖ **Fundamental Analysis Dos and Don'ts for Success:**
Uncover the dos and don'ts of fundamental analysis, providing practical guidelines to enhance your analytical skills. Learn how to conduct thorough research, avoid common pitfalls, and make well-informed

investment decisions.

❖ Benefits of Fundamental Analysis:

Gain insights into the myriad benefits of incorporating fundamental analysis into your trading strategy. Understand how a deep understanding of a company's financial health, market position, and growth prospects can contribute to long-term success.

❖ Risks of Fundamental Analysis:

Explore the potential challenges and risks associated with fundamental analysis. Acknowledge the limitations and pitfalls to effectively mitigate risks and make strategic adjustments in response to market uncertainties.

❖ Chapter Objective:

The primary objective of this chapter is to empower traders with the tools and knowledge necessary to conduct robust fundamental analysis. By delving into tokenomics, staying attuned to news and events, and mastering the dos and don'ts of fundamental analysis, traders will be well-equipped to navigate the complexities of financial markets. Furthermore, understanding the benefits and risks associated with fundamental analysis ensures a well-rounded and informed approach to trading, fostering self-reliance and success in the dynamic world of finance.

Tokenomics:

Understanding the economic fundamentals of a cryptocurrency—its supply, demand, and utility—forms the basis of fundamental analysis.

Understanding Tokenomics: The Economics of Cryptocurrencies

Tokenomics, a portmanteau of "token" and "economics," refers to the economic system and principles governing a cryptocurrency. It encompasses various factors, including the distribution, creation, and utilization of a cryptocurrency's native tokens. Here's a comprehensive guide to tokenomics:

Key Components of Tokenomics:

1. Token Supply:

Total Supply: The maximum number of tokens that can ever be created for a cryptocurrency. It defines the overall scarcity and inflationary/deflationary aspects of the token.

Circulating Supply: The number of tokens available in the market and actively traded. It excludes tokens held by the project team or locked in longterm contracts.

2. Token Distribution:

Initial Coin Offering (ICO): The process through which a cryptocurrency project raises funds by selling its native tokens to investors. ICOs often determine the initial distribution of tokens.

Airdrops: The free distribution of tokens to existing holders or potential users as a marketing strategy to promote awareness and adoption.

Token Reserves: Allocations of tokens held by the project team, foundation, or development fund for future development, marketing, partnerships, or other purposes.

3. Token Utility:

Use Cases: The practical applications of the cryptocurrency within its ecosystem. This could include using the token for transaction fees, governance, staking, access to specific features, or as a medium of exchange within a decentralized platform.

Smart Contracts: If the cryptocurrency operates on a blockchain that supports smart contracts, the utility of the token may extend to executing programmable agreements and decentralized applications (DApps).

4. Incentive Mechanisms:

Mining Rewards: For proofofwork blockchains, miners are rewarded with newly created tokens for validating transactions and securing the network.

Staking Rewards: In proofofstake or delegated proofofstake consensus mechanisms, users can earn rewards by holding and staking their tokens to support network operations.

Governance Participation: Some tokens provide voting rights, allowing holders to participate in the governance and decisionmaking processes of the network.

5. Token Burn and Buybacks:

Token Burn: The intentional and permanent removal of a certain number of tokens from circulation, usually done to reduce the overall supply and potentially increase scarcity.

Buybacks: Projects may use profits or reserved funds to buy back and burn tokens from the market, reducing supply and potentially influencing price.

6. Economic Model:

Inflationary vs. Deflationary: The choice between creating new tokens over time (inflationary) or reducing the token supply (deflationary) can impact the token's value and longterm viability.

Emission Schedule: The planned release of new tokens into circulation over time. This schedule can vary among different cryptocurrencies.

Practical Considerations:

1. Community Engagement:

A vibrant and engaged community is crucial for the success of a cryptocurrency. The tokenomics should incentivize community participation and support.

2. Transparency:

Clear and transparent communication about tokenomics is essential. Users and investors should have easy access to information about token supply, distribution, and the project's longterm plans.

3. Scalability:

The economic model should be scalable to accommodate the growth of the project and the increasing demand for the native token.

Common Mistakes to Avoid:

1. Unrealistic Token Supply:

Setting an unrealistic total supply or poorly distributing tokens can lead to issues such as excessive inflation or concentration of ownership.

2. Lack of Utility:

If a token lacks practical use cases within its ecosystem, it may struggle to gain adoption and maintain value.

3. Opaque Tokenomics:

Failing to provide clear and transparent information about tokenomics can erode trust within the community and hinder adoption.

Tokenomics is a foundational element of any cryptocurrency project, influencing its viability, adoption, and longterm success. A welldesigned tokenomics model aligns the interests of stakeholders, fosters community engagement, and ensures a sustainable economic system for the cryptocurrency. As the blockchain and cryptocurrency space evolves, careful consideration of tokenomics remains crucial for the development and growth of innovative projects.

Tokenomics Tips: Crafting a Strong Crypto Economy

Tokenomics plays a crucial role in the success and sustainability of a cryptocurrency project. Here are some dos and don'ts to consider when designing and implementing tokenomics:

Dos:

1. Clearly Define Token Utility:

Do: Clearly articulate the practical use cases of the token within the ecosystem. Whether it's for transactions, governance, staking, or accessing specific features, ensure that the utility aligns with the project's objectives.

2. Transparent Token Distribution:

Do: Be transparent about how tokens are distributed, including details about ICOs, airdrops, team allocations, and any reserved funds. Transparency builds trust among the community.

3. Incentive Mechanisms:

Do: Incorporate incentive mechanisms that encourage user participation, longterm holding, and contributions to the project. Incentives can include staking rewards, governance participation, or other engagementbased rewards.

4. Scalable Economic Model:

Do: Design an economic model that can scale with the growth of the project. Consider how the tokenomics will adapt to increased demand, user base, and ecosystem complexity.

5. Community Engagement:

Do: Foster a strong and engaged community. Create mechanisms for community involvement, feedback, and governance. An active and supportive community is often key to the success of a cryptocurrency project.

6. Dynamic Governance Structures:

Do: Implement dynamic governance structures that allow token holders to participate in decisionmaking processes. This can enhance decentralization and communitydriven development.

7. Token Burns and Buybacks:

Do: Consider mechanisms such as token burns or buybacks to reduce token supply over time. These practices can contribute to scarcity and potentially impact token value positively.

Don'ts:

1. Undefined Token Utility:

Don't: Introduce a token without a clear and practical purpose. Lack of utility can lead to low demand and hinder the longterm sustainability of the project.

2. Opaque Token Distribution:

Don't: Keep details of token distribution hidden or unclear. Lack of transparency can create suspicion and negatively impact the project's reputation.

3. Overly Complex Models:

Don't: Create overly complex tokenomics models that are difficult for users to understand. Complexity can lead to confusion and may deter potential investors or users.

4. Ignoring Community Feedback:

Don't: Disregard community feedback and preferences. The community is a valuable resource for insights and can provide feedback on potential improvements to tokenomics.

5. Relying Solely on Speculation:

Don't: Build a tokenomics model solely based on speculative factors. Consider real use cases, practical applications, and the longterm vision of the project.

6. Neglecting Security:

Don't: Neglect the security aspect of tokenomics. Ensure that smart contracts are secure, and vulnerabilities are addressed promptly to prevent potential exploits.

7. Ignoring Regulatory Considerations:

Don't: Disregard regulatory considerations. Stay informed about the regulatory landscape and ensure that the tokenomics model complies with relevant laws and guidelines.

Effective tokenomics is a balancing act that requires thoughtful consideration of various factors. By adhering to best practices, maintaining transparency, and actively engaging with the community, cryptocurrency projects can build sustainable token economies that contribute to longterm success. Regularly reassess and adapt tokenomics models to align with the evolving needs of the project and the broader crypto ecosystem.

News and Events:

Marketmoving events, partnerships, and regulatory developments can significantly impact cryptocurrency prices. Staying informed is key.

Mastering Cryptocurrency and Financial Market News Navigation

Staying informed about news and events is crucial for anyone involved in cryptocurrency, finance, and trading. Market sentiment, price movements, and investment decisions are often influenced by current events and developments. Here's a guide on how to navigate news and events in these dynamic markets:

Sources of News:

1. Crypto News Websites:

Websites dedicated to cryptocurrency news, such as CoinDesk, CoinTelegraph, and The Block, provide uptodate information on market trends, regulatory changes, and project updates.

2. Financial News Outlets:

Traditional financial news outlets like Bloomberg, CNBC, and Reuters cover global financial markets, including cryptocurrency. These platforms offer insights into broader economic trends that may impact digital assets.

3. Social Media:

Platforms like Twitter and Reddit are popular for realtime updates and discussions within the cryptocurrency community. However, it's essential to verify information from reliable sources.

4. Official Announcements:

Keep an eye on official announcements from cryptocurrency projects, regulatory bodies, and influential industry figures. These can provide insights into partnerships, technological developments, and regulatory changes.

5. Conferences and Events:

Attend cryptocurrency conferences and events to gain firsthand knowledge about industry trends, network with professionals, and hear keynote speakers share their perspectives.

Navigating News and Events:

1. Verify Information:

Due diligence is crucial. Verify information from multiple reliable sources before making decisions based on news or announcements. Misinformation can spread quickly in the fastpaced world of cryptocurrencies.

2. Understand Market Sentiment:

News and events can influence market sentiment. Positive developments may lead to a bullish market, while negative news can result in a bearish outlook. Stay attuned to market sentiment and be prepared for price reactions.

3. Economic Indicators:

Understand the impact of economic indicators on traditional financial markets, as these can also affect cryptocurrency prices. Key indicators include GDP growth, employment reports, and central bank decisions.

4. Regulatory Developments:

Regulatory news can significantly impact the cryptocurrency market. Stay informed about changes in regulations, potential bans, or regulatory frameworks being introduced in different countries.

5. Earnings Reports:

For traditional investments, such as stocks, pay attention to earnings reports of publicly traded companies. Positive or negative financial results can influence broader market trends.

Common Mistakes to Avoid

1. Reacting Impulsively:

Avoid making impulsive decisions based on breaking news. Take the time to analyze and understand the broader implications before taking action.

2. Ignoring Fundamental Analysis:

While news is important, consider combining it with fundamental analysis to gain a comprehensive understanding of the market conditions.

3. Disregarding Market Trends:

Understand the prevailing market trends and how they may be influenced by news and events. Ignoring the overall trend can lead to counterproductive trading decisions.

Dos and Don'ts of Navigating News and Events in Financial Markets

Staying informed about news and events is crucial in financial markets, including cryptocurrencies. Here are some dos and don'ts to help you navigate news and events effectively:

Dos:

1. Verify Information:

Do: Verify information from multiple reliable sources before making trading or investment decisions. Crossreferencing news helps reduce the risk of acting on misinformation.

2. Stay Informed About Economic Indicators:

Do: Stay informed about key economic indicators, such as GDP growth, employment reports, and interest rate decisions. These indicators can have a significant impact on traditional financial markets.

3. Understand Market Sentiment:

Do: Understand how news and events influence market sentiment. Positive developments may lead to a bullish market, while negative news can result in a bearish outlook. Consider sentiment in your decisionmaking process.

4. Diversify Information Sources:

Do: Diversify your sources of information. Relying on a variety of reputable news outlets, financial analysts, and official announcements provides a more comprehensive view of the market.

5. Consider Fundamental Analysis:

Do: Combine news analysis with fundamental analysis. Understanding the underlying factors that drive market movements can enhance your decisionmaking process.

6. Attend Conferences and Events:

Do: Attend industry conferences and events to gain firsthand knowledge, network with professionals, and stay updated on the latest developments. Conferences can provide valuable insights that may not be immediately apparent in news articles.

Don'ts:

1. React Impulsively:

Don't: React impulsively to breaking news. Take the time to analyze the information, consider the broader context, and assess potential implications before making decisions.

2. Disregard Market Trends:

Don't: Disregard prevailing market trends. While news and events can influence shortterm movements, understanding the overall trend is essential for making informed trading decisions.

3. Ignore Economic Calendar:

Don't: Ignore the economic calendar. Economic events, such as central bank announcements or earnings reports, are often scheduled and can be anticipated. Stay aware of upcoming events that may impact the markets.

4. Overreact to ShortTerm Fluctuations:

Don't: Overreact to shortterm market fluctuations. Focus on the longterm trends and objectives of your investment strategy rather than being swayed by momentary market reactions.

5. Neglect Risk Management:

Don't: Neglect risk management principles. Even in the face of significant news events, having a welldefined risk management strategy helps protect your capital and minimize potential losses.

6. Disregard Regulatory Changes:

Don't: Disregard regulatory changes. Stay informed about evolving regulatory landscapes, especially in the cryptocurrency space, as they can have a profound impact on market dynamics.

Navigating news and events in financial markets requires a balanced and informed approach. By verifying information, understanding market sentiment, considering fundamental factors, and staying disciplined in your decisionmaking process, you can better position yourself to make sound investment choices. Remember to adapt to changing market conditions and maintain a strategic, longterm perspective.

Fundamental analysis Dos and Don'ts for Success

Fundamental analysis plays a crucial role in making informed investment decisions in the cryptocurrency market. Here are the dos and don'ts, as well as the benefits and risks associated with fundamental analysis.

Do: Conduct Comprehensive Research

Project Whitepapers: Dive into the whitepapers of cryptocurrencies to understand the technology, use case, and the problem they aim to solve.

Team Background: Investigate the background and expertise of the development team. A strong and experienced team can contribute to the success of a project.

Market Potential: Assess the market potential of the cryptocurrency. Consider the realworld applications and demand for the project.

Don't: Neglect Market Trends

Ignoring Market Trends: While focusing on individual projects, don't ignore broader market trends and sentiments. External factors can influence the success of a cryptocurrency.

Overlooking Regulatory Environment: Neglecting the regulatory environment can lead to unexpected legal challenges for a project. Stay informed about the regulatory landscape.

Ignoring Community Sentiment: The sentiment of the cryptocurrency community can impact a project's success. Monitor social media, forums, and news for community reactions.

Benefits of Fundamental Analysis

LongTerm Investment: Fundamental analysis is essential for identifying cryptocurrencies with strong fundamentals, making it suitable for longterm investors.

Understanding Value: It helps investors understand the intrinsic value of a cryptocurrency, which can be crucial in assessing its longterm viability.

Risk Mitigation: By evaluating the project's fundamentals, investors can make more informed decisions, reducing the risk of investing in projects with weak foundations.

Risks of Fundamental Analysis

Subjectivity: Different investors may interpret fundamental data differently, leading to subjective conclusions about a project's potential.

Market Timing: Fundamental analysis may not provide precise timing for market entry or exit. It's more suited for longterm investors than shortterm traders.

Unforeseen Events: External events, such as technological breakthroughs or regulatory changes, can impact projects unexpectedly, making predictions challenging.

CHAPTER 4

RISK MANAGEMENT AND PSYCHOLOGY

In "Trade Phenomena: The Path to Self-Reliance," Chapter 4 delves into the crucial aspects of Risk Management and Psychology, offering readers an indispensable guide to navigate the intricate intersection of disciplined decision-making and the psychological aspects of trading.

❖ Position Sizing:

Uncover the strategic importance of position sizing in optimizing risk and returns. Learn how to calculate the appropriate amount of capital to allocate to each trade, ensuring that your risk exposure aligns with your overall trading goals. Practical insights into position sizing empower you to strike the right balance between risk and reward.

❖ Emotional Discipline:

Explore the psychological dimensions of trading and cultivate emotional discipline. This section provides actionable strategies to manage emotions such as fear and greed, enabling traders to make rational decisions even in the face of market volatility. Develop a resilient mindset that withstands the emotional challenges inherent in the trading journey.

❖ Risk Management Dos and Don'ts for Success:

Gain a comprehensive understanding of effective risk management strategies. Discover dos and don'ts that guide you in protecting your capital and minimizing potential losses. Insights from successful traders illuminate the path to responsible risk management, offering valuable lessons for both novice and experienced investors.

❖ Psychology Dos and Don'ts for Success:

Delve into the psychological aspects of trading success. Learn dos and don'ts that are essential for maintaining a healthy and constructive mindset. Understanding the psychological pitfalls and best practices empowers traders to make informed decisions, navigate market fluctuations, and foster a positive trading experience.

❖ Pioneer Trading Strategies:

Concluding the chapter, explore pioneering trading strategies that have withstood the test of time. Drawing inspiration from successful traders of the past, this section provides insights into timeless approaches that align with the principles of self-reliant trading. Uncover the strategies that form the bedrock of sustained success in the dynamic world of financial markets.

Chapter 4 serves as a comprehensive guide, equipping readers with the knowledge and tools needed to master the critical elements of risk management and psychology. Whether you're a seasoned trader or just beginning your journey, this chapter provides actionable insights that contribute to building a resilient and self-reliant trading mindset.

Position Sizing:

Effectively managing risk involves determining the appropriate size for each position, mitigating potential losses.

Position Sizing: A Key Element of Risk Management in Trading

Position sizing is a critical aspect of risk management in trading that involves determining the amount of capital to allocate to a specific trade. Proper position sizing helps traders manage risk, preserve capital, and optimize the potential for longterm success. Here's a comprehensive guide on position sizing:

Definition:

Position sizing refers to the process of determining the number of units or contracts to trade in a particular investment. It is designed to control the amount of risk exposure in a trade and aligns with an individual trader's risk tolerance and overall trading strategy.

Key Components of Position Sizing:

1. Risk Tolerance:

Before entering a trade, traders need to define their risk tolerance, which is the maximum amount of capital they are willing to risk on a single trade. This is often expressed as a percentage of the trading capital.

2. StopLoss Placement:

The placement of a stoploss order is crucial in position sizing. It defines the point at which a trade will be exited to limit potential losses. The distance between the entry point and the stoploss level influences position size.

3. Volatility:

Volatility measures the magnitude of price fluctuations. Traders may adjust their position size based on the volatility of the asset. Higher volatility may warrant smaller position sizes to accommodate larger price swings.

4. Account Size:

The total capital in a trading account influences position sizing. Traders typically avoid risking a large percentage of their total account capital on a single trade.

Position Sizing Strategies:

1. Fixed Dollar Amount:

Traders allocate a fixed dollar amount or percentage of their trading capital to each trade. This method keeps the risk consistent across different trades.

2. Percent of Trading Capital:

Traders determine the position size based on a percentage of their total trading capital. For example, risking 2% of the total capital on a single trade.

3. Volatility Based Sizing:

Position size is adjusted based on the historical volatility of the asset. Higher volatility may result in smaller position sizes to account for larger potential price swings.

4. Risk Adjusted Position Sizing:

This method considers both the distance to the stoploss level and the volatility of the asset. The position size is adjusted to maintain a consistent level of risk across different market conditions.

Practical Application:

1. Calculate Position Size:

Use the formula: $$\text{Position Size} = \frac{\text{Risk per Trade}}{\text{StopLoss Distance}}$$

2. Diversify Positions:

Avoid concentrating too much capital in a single position. Diversifying across multiple assets or trades can help manage risk.

3. Adjust Position Size for Market Conditions:

Consider the prevailing market conditions, volatility, and any recent news or events that may impact the asset. Adjust position sizes accordingly.

Common Mistakes to Avoid:

1. Ignoring Risk Tolerance:

Failing to define and adhere to a predetermined risk tolerance can lead to excessive risktaking and potential large losses.

2. Overleveraging:

Allocating too much capital to a single trade can lead to overleveraging, increasing the risk of significant losses.

3. Not Considering Market Conditions:

Ignoring current market conditions and volatility may result in inappropriate position sizes for the level of risk desired.

Position sizing is a crucial element of risk management in trading. By carefully determining the amount of capital to allocate to each trade based on risk tolerance, stoploss placement, and market conditions, traders can protect their capital and optimize their chances of longterm success. Implementing a disciplined position sizing strategy is key to achieving consistency and sustainability in trading.

Dos and Don'ts of Position Sizing in Trading

Effective position sizing is a crucial aspect of risk management in trading. Here are some dos and don'ts to consider when determining the size of your positions:

Dos:

1. Define Your Risk Tolerance:

Do: Clearly define your risk tolerance before entering a trade. Determine the maximum percentage of your trading capital that you are willing to risk on a single trade.

2. Set StopLoss Orders:

Do: Always use stoploss orders to limit potential losses. Determine where you will exit the trade if it moves against you, and place a stoploss order accordingly.

3. Calculate Position Size:

Do: Calculate your position size based on the predetermined risk per trade and the distance to your stoploss level. The position size formula is: $$ \text{Position Size} = \frac{\text{Risk per Trade}}{\text{StopLoss Distance}} $$

4. Diversify Your Portfolio:

Do: Diversify your positions to avoid concentration risk. Avoid putting too much capital into a single trade or asset, as this can help spread risk across different assets.

5. Adapt Position Size to Volatility:

Do: Consider adjusting your position size based on the volatility of the asset. In more volatile markets, smaller position sizes may be appropriate to account for larger price swings.

6. Review and Adjust:

Do: Regularly review and adjust your position sizes based on changes in market conditions, your account size, and risk tolerance. Flexibility is key to adapting to evolving circumstances.

7. Use a Consistent Approach:

Do: Use a consistent position sizing approach across your trades. This helps maintain a structured and disciplined risk management strategy.

Don'ts:

1. Ignore StopLoss Levels:

Don't: Ignore or neglect setting stoploss levels. Failing to use stoploss orders can expose you to significant losses if a trade moves against you.

2. Risk Too Much Per Trade:

Don't: Risk an excessive percentage of your trading capital on a single trade. This can lead to substantial losses and jeopardize the overall health of your trading account.

3. Neglect Market Conditions:

Don't: Neglect considering current market conditions. Adjust your position sizes based on the prevailing volatility, trends, and other relevant factors.

4. Overleverage:

Don't: Overleverage your positions. Avoid allocating too much leverage, as it can amplify both gains and losses and increase the risk of a margin call.

5. Revenge Trading:

Don't: Engage in revenge trading by increasing your position size after a losing trade to recover losses quickly. This can lead to further losses and emotional decisionmaking.

6. Disregard Portfolio Diversification:

Don't: Put all your capital into a single asset or trade. Diversification helps spread risk and reduces the impact of a poorperforming asset on your overall portfolio.

7. Rely on Gut Feeling:

Don't: Rely solely on gut feeling or intuition for position sizing. Use a systematic and calculated approach based on your predetermined risk parameters.

Position sizing is a critical element of successful trading. By following these dos and don'ts, traders can implement a disciplined and riskconscious approach to position sizing, contributing to more consistent and sustainable trading outcomes. Always prioritize risk management as an integral part of your overall trading strategy.

Emotional Discipline:

Psychological factors play a crucial role in trading. Emotional discipline helps traders make rational decisions even in the face of market fluctuations.

Emotional Discipline in Trading: Mastering Market Psychology

Emotional discipline, often referred to as emotional control or psychological discipline, is a fundamental aspect of successful trading. It involves managing and mastering one's emotions to make rational, wellinformed decisions in the dynamic and often unpredictable world of financial markets. Here's a comprehensive guide on cultivating emotional discipline in trading:

Understanding Emotional Discipline:

1. Emotional Intelligence:

Emotional discipline is rooted in emotional intelligence, which involves recognizing, understanding, and managing one's own emotions and the emotions of others. In trading, this means being aware of how emotions can impact decisionmaking.

2. Common Emotional Challenges in Trading:

Greed: The desire for excessive profits.
Fear: The fear of losses or missing out on opportunities.
Hope: Unrealistic optimism or holding onto losing positions.
Regret: Dwelling on past mistakes or missed opportunities.

Key Principles of Emotional Discipline:

1. Developing a Trading Plan:

A welldefined trading plan provides a structured framework, reducing the likelihood of impulsive decisions driven by emotions. It should include entry and exit criteria, risk management rules, and clear goals.

2. Setting Realistic Expectations:

Understanding that losses are inevitable and part of the trading process helps in setting realistic expectations. Unrealistic expectations can lead to emotional turmoil when faced with inevitable challenges.

3. Risk Management:

Implementing effective risk management strategies, such as setting stoploss orders and position sizing, helps limit potential losses. This, in turn, reduces the emotional impact of adverse market movements.

4. Maintaining Objectivity:

Detaching oneself emotionally from trades and making decisions based on facts and analysis, rather than emotional reactions, is crucial. Objectivity prevents impulsive actions driven by fear or greed.

5. Learning from Mistakes:

Instead of dwelling on mistakes, view them as opportunities for learning and improvement. Analyzing past trades objectively helps refine strategies and avoid repeating errors.

Practical Tips for Emotional Discipline:

1. Mindfulness and Awareness:

Cultivate mindfulness to stay present in the moment and be aware of your emotions. Regular selfreflection helps identify emotional patterns and triggers.

2. Take Breaks:

If feeling overwhelmed or emotional, taking a break from trading can be beneficial. Stepping away allows time to regain composure and approach decisions with a clear mind.

3. Journaling:

Maintain a trading journal to record thoughts, emotions, and the rationale behind each trade. Reviewing the journal can provide insights into emotional patterns and areas for improvement.

4. Visualization:

Visualize successful trades and positive outcomes. Positive visualization can help create a constructive mindset and reduce anxiety.

5. Seeking Support:

Engage with a trading community or mentor to share experiences and gain perspectives. Discussing challenges with others can provide valuable insights and emotional support.

Common Emotional Discipline Mistakes:

1. Ignoring Emotional Signals:

Ignoring or suppressing emotions can be detrimental. Acknowledge emotional signals and work towards understanding and managing them.

2. Revenge Trading:

Seeking revenge after a loss by making impulsive trades to recover can lead to further losses. It's essential to recognize and avoid revenge trading.

3. Overconfidence:

Overconfidence can result in excessive risktaking and failure to adhere to trading plans. Regularly assess and reassess your skills and strategies to avoid complacency.

Emotional discipline is a continuous journey of selfawareness and selfimprovement for traders. Mastering the psychology of the markets is as important as understanding market analysis and technical indicators. By developing emotional discipline, traders can navigate the challenges of trading with resilience, make better decisions, and increase the likelihood of longterm success in the dynamic world of financial markets.

Risk Management Dos and Don'ts for Success

Effective risk management and a disciplined psychological approach are essential for success in the dynamic and often unpredictable world of cryptocurrency trading. Here are the dos and don'ts to help you navigate the challenges associated with risk management and maintain a healthy trading psychology.

Risk Management Dos:

1. Set Clear Stop Loss Orders: Determine in advance the maximum amount of loss you are willing to tolerate on a trade. Set clear stop loss orders to automatically execute when predefined levels are reached.

2. Diversify Your Portfolio: Spread your investments across different assets to reduce the impact of a poor performing asset on your overall portfolio. Diversification helps manage risk exposure.

3. Allocate a Percentage of Your Portfolio: Determine a specific percentage of your total portfolio that you are comfortable risking on any single trade. This ensures that no single trade can disproportionately impact your overall investment.

4. Regularly Reevaluate Your Risk Tolerance: As market conditions change or your financial situation evolves, regularly reassess your risk tolerance. Adjust your position sizes and risk per trade accordingly.

5. Use Position Sizing: Adjust the size of your positions based on the level of risk associated with each trade. Larger positions may be appropriate for low risk trades, while smaller positions are suitable for higher risk trades.

Risk Management Don'ts:

1. Ignore Stop Loss Orders: Resist the temptation to override or ignore stop loss orders in the hope that the market will reverse. Stick to your predetermined risk levels.

2. Invest More Than You Can Afford to Lose: Never invest more than you can afford to lose. Cryptocurrency markets can be highly volatile, and it's essential to protect your capital.

3. Chase Losses: Avoid increasing your position size to recover losses from previous trades. Chasing losses can lead to a cycle of emotional decisionmaking and increased risk.

4. Neglect Risk Reward Ratios: Assess the potential reward against the potential risk before entering a trade. Avoid trades where the potential loss outweighs the potential gain.

5. Become Overconfident: A string of successful trades can lead to overconfidence. Stay disciplined and adhere to your risk management plan, regardless of recent performance.

Psychology Dos and Don'ts for Success

Psychological Dos:

1. Stay Emotionally Disciplined: Cultivate emotional discipline to avoid making impulsive decisions based on fear or greed. Stick to your trading plan.

2. Take Breaks: Step away from the screen when feeling overwhelmed or stressed. Taking breaks helps clear your mind and maintain focus.

3. Learn from Mistakes: View losses as opportunities for learning rather than failures. Analyze your mistakes, adjust your strategy, and continually improve.

4. Practice Patience: Successful trading requires patience. Wait for optimal setups, and don't feel compelled to trade in every market condition.

5. Focus on Process, Not Just Outcome: Concentrate on executing your trading strategy correctly rather than being solely results oriented. A well-executed plan, even with losses, is a step towards success.

Psychological Don'ts:

1. Ignore Stress Signals: If stress levels become overwhelming, do not ignore them. Seek support or take a break to avoid making decisions under emotional duress.

2. Gamble or Speculate: Trading is not gambling. Avoid speculative behavior and instead, base your decisions on well researched strategies.

3. Compare Yourself to Others: Avoid comparing your success or failure to others in the market. Each trader's journey is unique, and comparisons can lead to unwarranted emotional pressure.

4. Trade Without a Plan: Never enter a trade without a well-defined plan. Impulsive actions can lead to regrettable decisions and increased emotional stress.

5. Neglect Mental Wellbeing: Prioritize your mental wellbeing. Neglecting mental health can impair decisionmaking and hinder overall trading performance.

By incorporating these dos and don'ts into your risk management and trading psychology, you can build a solid foundation for success in the cryptocurrency market. Remember that consistent discipline and a strategic approach are key to navigating the challenges of trading.

Happy Trading!

CHAPTER 5

PIONEER TRADING STRATEGIES

Embark on a captivating journey through the annals of financial history as "Trade Phenomena: The Path to Self-Reliance" unfolds the remarkable strategies employed by legendary figures who pioneered the world of trading. In this illuminating chapter, we delve into the timeless wisdom of iconic traders whose innovative approaches have left an indelible mark on the financial landscape.

❖ **Historical Strategies by Historical Figures:**

- **Jesse Livermore (1877–1940):** Explore the trading brilliance of one of the most famous stock traders of all time, known for his mastery of market trends and understanding of crowd psychology.

- **George Soros (b. 1930):** Uncover the insights of the hedge fund titan renowned for his groundbreaking theories on reflexivity and his historic bet against the British pound.

- **Paul Tudor Jones (b. 1954):** Navigate the strategies of the hedge fund manager and philanthropist, famous for predicting the 1987 stock market crash.

- **John Templeton (1912–2008):** Learn from the contrarian investor and mutual fund pioneer who sought opportunities in times of market pessimism.

- **Ray Dalio (b. 1949):** Discover the principles of the founder of Bridgewater Associates, known for his systematic and innovative investment strategies.

- **Richard Dennis (1949–2018):** Explore the Turtle Trader's experiment and the trend-following strategies that became legendary in the world of commodities trading.

- **Ed Seykota (b. 1946):** Delve into the systematic trend-following techniques of this trading pioneer and technical analysis expert.
- **Nicolas Darvas (1920–1977):** Unearth the unique trading techniques of the dancer-turned-trader who gained fame for his momentum-based strategy.
- **Bernard Baruch (1870–1965):** Absorb the wisdom of the adviser to presidents, known for his astute market analysis and investment strategies.
- **William J. O'Neil (1933–2019):** Explore the innovative and growth-focused strategies of the founder of Investor's Business Daily.

❖ **Effective Strategies by Cryptocurrency Professionals:**

Delve into the modern era with insights from cryptocurrency professionals who have navigated the dynamic and decentralized world of digital assets. Gain valuable perspectives from industry leaders shaping the future of finance.

- **Changpeng Zhao - @cz_binance:** Explore the strategies of the visionary founder of Binance, a global cryptocurrency exchange.
- **Satoshi Nakamoto:** Uncover the mysterious and groundbreaking strategies of the pseudonymous creator of Bitcoin, whose innovative whitepaper laid the foundation for the entire cryptocurrency ecosystem.
- **Brian Armstrong - @brian_armstrong:** Learn from the CEO of Coinbase, a key player in the cryptocurrency space, and his effective strategies in navigating the evolving market.
- **Chris Larsen - @chrislarsensf:** Gain insights from the co-founder of Ripple and his impact on the development of blockchain-based financial solutions.
- **Tyler and Cameron Winklevoss - @tyler and @cameron:** Explore the strategies of the Winklevoss twins, co-founders of Gemini, a leading cryptocurrency exchange.
- **Mike Novogratz - @novogratz:** Discover the strategies of the former hedge fund manager turned cryptocurrency investor and founder of Galaxy Digital.
- **Joseph Lubin - @ethereumJoseph:** Understand the strategies of the co-founder of Ethereum and his contributions to the development of decentralized applications.
- **Micree Zhan - @MicreeZ:** Explore the innovative strategies of the co-founder of Bitmain, a prominent player in the cryptocurrency mining industry.

- **Vitalik Buterin - @VitalikButerin:** Gain insights from the co-founder of Ethereum and his role in shaping the landscape of blockchain technology.
- **Matthew Roszak - @matthewroszak:** Learn from the strategies of the blockchain entrepreneur and co-founder of Bloq.

This chapter serves as a bridge between the historical foundations of trading and the innovative strategies employed by cryptocurrency professionals, providing readers with a comprehensive understanding of the diverse and evolving world of financial markets.

Historical Strategies by historical figures

Several historical figures are recognized for their success as traders, making significant contributions to the financial markets. Here are some notable historical successful traders:

1. Jesse Livermore (1877–1940):

Overview: Often considered one of the greatest stock traders in history, Jesse Livermore is known for his speculative trading in the early 20th century. He made and lost fortunes multiple times, gaining fame for predicting market crashes, including the 1929 Great Depression.

Key Lessons: Livermore emphasized the importance of understanding market psychology, trend analysis, and disciplined risk management.

Trading strategies

Jesse Livermore, one of the greatest traders in history, developed trading strategies that allowed him to amass and lose several fortunes during his career. Livermore's trading principles are outlined in his book, "Reminiscences of a Stock Operator," and are still studied and discussed by traders today. Here are some key trading strategies associated with Jesse Livermore:

1. Trend Following:

- **Principle:** Livermore was a strong advocate of following the trend. He believed that the trend was a powerful force that should not be ignored.
- **Strategy:** Livermore would enter positions in the direction of the prevailing trend and hold onto them until signs of a reversal emerged. He often used technical analysis to identify trends and potential turning points.

2. Reading Market Sentiment:

- **Principle:** Livermore emphasized the importance of understanding market sentiment and the psychology of other market participants.
- **Strategy:** Livermore closely observed price action, volume, and market dynamics to gauge the sentiment of traders. He paid attention to how the market reacted to news and events, looking for signs of accumulation or distribution.

3. Avoiding Overtrading:

- **Principle:** Livermore warned against excessive trading, emphasizing the importance of patience and discipline.
- **Strategy:** Livermore would wait for high-probability setups and avoid making trades simply for the sake of being in the market. He

understood the significance of waiting for the right opportunities.

4. Cutting Losses Quickly:

- **Principle:** Livermore was a firm believer in cutting losses quickly to protect capital and avoid significant drawdowns.
- **Strategy:** Livermore used stop-loss orders to limit losses on his trades. If a trade moved against him, he would exit the position promptly to prevent further losses.

5. Pyramiding:

- **Principle:** Livermore employed a strategy known as pyramiding, where he added to winning positions to maximize profits.
- **Strategy:** When Livermore's trades moved in his favor, he would add to his positions to capitalize on the trend's strength. Pyramiding allowed him to compound his gains during strong market moves.

6. Concentration:

- **Principle:** Livermore believed in concentrating his capital on his best ideas when the market conditions were favorable.
- **Strategy:** Livermore would focus on a limited number of stocks or sectors that showed the strongest trends. By concentrating his capital, he aimed to maximize returns during favorable market conditions.

7. Being Adaptive:

- **Principle:** Livermore stressed the importance of being adaptable and adjusting strategies based on changing market conditions.
- **Strategy:** Livermore would reassess his trading approach as market dynamics evolved. He recognized that strategies that worked in one market environment might need adjustments in another.

8. Understanding the Role of News:

- **Principle:** Livermore understood the impact of news and events on market sentiment.
- **Strategy:** While Livermore used technical analysis, he also paid attention to news and events that could influence market sentiment. Understanding how the market reacted to news was an integral part of his strateg.

9. Keeping Emotions in Check:

- **Principle:** Livermore was aware of the emotional challenges in trading and emphasized the need to control emotions.
- **Strategy:** Livermore practiced emotional discipline, avoiding impulsive decisions driven by fear or greed. He maintained a calm and rational approach to trading.

It's important to note that while Livermore's trading strategies were successful for him, trading always involves risks, and what worked in the past may not necessarily work in the future. Traders should carefully consider their risk tolerance and adapt strategies to their own trading styles and market conditions. Livermore's legacy lies not only in his strategies but also in the lessons he shared about market psychology and risk management.

◆◆◆

2. George Soros (b. 1930):

Overview: A Hungarian-American investor and philanthropist, George Soros is known for his success in currency speculation. In 1992, he famously "broke the Bank of England" by shorting the British pound, earning around $1 billion in profits.

Key Lessons: Soros is known for his theory of reflexivity, which suggests that market participants' perceptions can influence market fundamentals.

Trading strategies

George Soros, a Hungarian-American investor and philanthropist, gained fame for his successful currency speculation and investment strategies. While Soros' approach is multifaceted, there are key principles and strategies associated with his trading philosophy. Here are some notable aspects of George Soros' trading strategies:

1. Reflexivity:

- **Principle:** Soros developed the theory of reflexivity, which asserts that market participants' perceptions and actions can influence market fundamentals. In other words, the actions of investors can impact the very market conditions they are reacting to.

- **Strategy:** Soros used reflexivity as a guiding principle, seeking to identify situations where market participants' beliefs created self-reinforcing trends. He would then position himself to capitalize on these trends.

2. Global Macro Investing:

- **Principle:** Soros is a prominent figure in global macro investing, where investors analyze and make bets on broad economic trends and events across various asset classes and countries.

- **Strategy:** Soros would take a macroeconomic view of the world, considering factors such as interest rates, inflation, and geopolitical events. His trades often involved currencies, commodities, and equities, allowing him to profit from global trends.

3. Shorting Currencies:

- **Principle:** Soros is famous for "breaking the Bank of England" in 1992 when he successfully speculated against the British pound, leading to a significant devaluation.
- **Strategy:** Soros identified situations where currencies were overvalued or facing pressure, and he would take large short positions. His success in the currency markets contributed to his reputation as a legendary trader.

4. Risk Management:

- **Principle:** Soros emphasized the importance of managing risk and protecting capital. He believed in staying flexible and adjusting positions based on changing market conditions.
- **Strategy:** Soros would use stop-loss orders to limit losses on his trades. Additionally, he would reassess and adjust his positions if market conditions evolved differently from his initial expectations.

5. Quantitative Analysis:

- **Principle:** While Soros is known for his macroeconomic approach, he also recognized the value of quantitative analysis and market research.
- **Strategy:** Soros and his team conducted in-depth research, analyzing economic data, market indicators, and trends. This comprehensive analysis contributed to the formulation of his trading strategies.

6. Aggressive Position Sizing:

- **Principle:** Soros was known for aggressive position sizing when he had high conviction in a trade.
- **Strategy:** When Soros had a strong belief in a market move, he would allocate a significant portion of his capital to that trade. This approach allowed him to maximize profits during favorable market conditions.

7. Adaptability:

- **Principle:** Soros emphasized the need for traders to adapt to changing market conditions and be willing to revise their views.
- **Strategy:** Soros was known for being flexible and open to changing his positions based on new information. He recognized that markets are dynamic, and successful trading requires adaptation.

8. Market Sentiment Analysis:

- **Principle:** Soros paid close attention to market sentiment and the behavior of other market participants.

- **Strategy:** Soros believed that understanding how the market perceived certain events or conditions was crucial. He would observe market reactions to news and events to gauge sentiment and make informed decisions.

9. Political and Economic Analysis:

- **Principle:** Soros integrated political and economic analysis into his trading decisions.
- **Strategy:** Soros considered the impact of political events and economic policies on financial markets. His ability to anticipate and react to changes in political landscapes contributed to his success.

It's important to note that Soros' trading strategies were unique to his style and expertise. While his methods can provide insights, traders should exercise caution and adapt strategies to their own risk tolerance, market understanding, and preferences. Soros' success also underscores the importance of continuous learning, adaptability, and a deep understanding of the interplay between markets and broader economic factors.

3. Paul Tudor Jones (b. 1954):

Overview: Paul Tudor Jones is an American hedge fund manager and philanthropist. He gained fame for predicting the 1987 stock market crash and successfully navigating various market cycles. Jones is the founder of Tudor Investment Corporation.

Key Lessons: Jones emphasizes the importance of risk management, trend following, and the psychological aspect of trading.

Trading strategies

Paul Tudor Jones, an American hedge fund manager, is renowned for his macro trading strategies and ability to navigate various market cycles. Here are key principles and trading strategies associated with Paul Tudor Jones:

1. Global Macro Investing:

- **Principle:** Jones is a prominent figure in global macro investing, focusing on significant economic trends and events that span across various asset classes and regions.
- **Strategy:** Jones analyzes macroeconomic factors such as interest rates, inflation, and geopolitical events to identify opportunities. His trading decisions are often based on his outlook for the broader economic environment.

2. Trend Following:

- **Principle:** Jones places a strong emphasis on trend following, believing that trends have the potential to persist for extended periods.

- **Strategy:** Jones looks for established trends and seeks to align his trades with these trends. He often uses technical analysis to identify trend reversals and entry points.

3. Risk Management:

- **Principle:** Jones is known for his disciplined approach to risk management, emphasizing the importance of preserving capital.
- **Strategy:** Jones uses stop-loss orders to limit potential losses on trades. He carefully manages position sizes to ensure that no single trade has a disproportionately large impact on his overall portfolio.

4. Top-Down Analysis:

- **Principle:** Jones employs a top-down approach to analysis, starting with a broad assessment of the macroeconomic environment before narrowing down to specific trades.
- **Strategy:** Jones first forms a macroeconomic view and then drills down into individual asset classes or securities that align with his outlook. This approach helps him allocate capital effectively.

5. Contrarian Views:

- **Principle:** Jones is known for taking contrarian views, often positioning himself against prevailing market sentiment.
- **Strategy:** When Jones believes that the market is overly optimistic or pessimistic, he may take positions that go against the consensus. This contrarian approach allows him to capitalize on market mispricing.

6. Quantitative Analysis:

- **Principle:** Jones integrates quantitative analysis into his decision-making process.
- **Strategy:** Jones uses quantitative models and data analysis to complement his macroeconomic views. This quantitative approach helps him identify potential opportunities and assess risk.

7. Liquidity Considerations:

- **Principle:** Jones pays attention to liquidity factors when making trading decisions.
- **Strategy:** Jones considers the liquidity of the markets or assets he trades. Liquidity can impact the ease of entering or exiting positions, and he adjusts his strategies accordingly.

8. Mental Flexibility:

- **Principle:** Jones emphasizes the importance of mental flexibility and adaptability in trading.

- **Strategy:** Jones understands that markets are dynamic, and being able to adapt to changing conditions is crucial. He reassesses his views and adjusts his positions when necessary.

9. Timing and Patience:
- **Principle:** Jones recognizes the significance of timing and exercises patience in waiting for the right market conditions.
- **Strategy:** Jones waits for high-probability setups and does not force trades. He understands that timing is crucial, and being patient allows him to enter trades when the risk-reward ratio is favorable.

10. Focus on Psychology:
- **Principle:** Jones acknowledges the psychological aspects of trading.
- **Strategy:** Jones pays attention to market psychology, investor sentiment, and the impact of emotions on trading decisions. Understanding these factors helps him navigate market dynamics.

It's important to note that while these strategies are associated with Paul Tudor Jones, successful trading requires careful consideration of individual risk tolerance, market conditions, and ongoing adaptation. Traders can draw inspiration from successful figures like Jones but should tailor their strategies to their own preferences and circumstances.

4. John Templeton (1912–2008):

Overview: Sir John Templeton was an American-born British investor and fund manager. He is known for founding the Templeton Growth Fund and for his contrarian approach to investing. Templeton achieved significant success in global equity markets.

Key Lessons: Templeton advocated a value investing approach, searching for undervalued assets and taking a long-term view on investments.

Trading strategies

John Templeton, a legendary investor and mutual fund pioneer, was known for his value investing philosophy. While Templeton was not a trader in the traditional sense, his investment strategies and principles influenced many in the financial industry. Here are key aspects of John Templeton's investment approach:

1. Value Investing:
- **Philosophy:** Templeton was a staunch advocate of value investing, focusing on the intrinsic value of assets.

- **Strategy:** He sought to identify stocks or assets that were trading below their intrinsic value. Templeton believed that markets sometimes mispriced assets, presenting opportunities for patient investors.

2. Contrarian Approach:

- **Philosophy:** Templeton often took a contrarian approach, investing in assets that were unpopular or out of favor with the market.
- **Strategy:** He believed that markets could be overly pessimistic or optimistic about certain assets, creating opportunities for investors who were willing to go against the prevailing sentiment.

3. Global Diversification:

- **Philosophy:** Templeton advocated for global diversification, emphasizing the importance of investing in a wide range of countries and regions.
- **Strategy:** He believed that opportunities existed globally, and by diversifying across countries and industries, investors could reduce risk and enhance potential returns.

4. Long-Term Perspective:

- **Philosophy:** Templeton was known for his long-term investment horizon, looking beyond short-term market fluctuations.
- **Strategy:** He encouraged investors to adopt a patient and disciplined approach, focusing on the fundamental value of assets over the long term.

5. Bottom-Up Stock Selection:

- **Philosophy:** Templeton engaged in bottom-up stock selection, evaluating individual companies rather than making broad market predictions.
- **Strategy:** He conducted thorough research on companies, analyzing financial statements, management quality, and growth prospects. This approach allowed him to identify undervalued stocks with strong potential.

6. Active Management:

- **Philosophy:** Templeton believed in active management and the potential for skilled fund managers to add value through security selection.
- **Strategy:** He managed the Templeton Growth Fund actively, making strategic investment decisions based on his analysis of individual securities and market conditions.

7. Behavioral Factors:

- **Philosophy:** Templeton acknowledged the role of behavioral factors in investment decisions.
- **Strategy:** He understood that market participants could be influenced by emotions such as fear and greed. By staying rational and disciplined, Templeton aimed to capitalize on mispricings driven by these emotional factors.

8. Risk Management:

- **Philosophy:** While seeking value, Templeton was mindful of risk and the importance of managing it effectively.
- **Strategy:** He diversified his portfolio to reduce company-specific risk and geographic risk. Additionally, Templeton carefully assessed the financial health and stability of the companies in which he invested.

9. Investing with Conviction:

- **Philosophy:** Templeton believed in investing with conviction when opportunities aligned with his research and analysis.
- **Strategy:** He was not afraid to take significant positions in assets he believed were undervalued, showcasing confidence in his investment decisions.

10. Active Research and Continuous Learning:

- **Philosophy:** Templeton valued ongoing research and learning in the investment process.
- **Strategy:** He stayed informed about global economic trends, political developments, and market conditions. This commitment to continuous learning contributed to his success over the years.

While Templeton's strategies are more aligned with long-term investing rather than short-term trading, his principles have had a profound impact on the investment community. Investors and traders alike can draw inspiration from Templeton's disciplined approach, focus on intrinsic value, and commitment to global diversification.

◆◆◆

5. Ray Dalio (b. 1949):

Overview: Ray Dalio is an American billionaire hedge fund manager and the founder of Bridgewater Associates, one of the world's largest hedge funds. Dalio is known for his macroeconomic and systematic investment approach.

Key Lessons: Dalio emphasizes the importance of understanding economic cycles, managing risk through diversification, and maintaining an open-minded approach.

Trading strategies

Ray Dalio, the founder of Bridgewater Associates, is known for his unique investment philosophy and systematic approach to trading. While Bridgewater Associates operates primarily as a hedge fund engaged in macro investing and risk management, Dalio's principles can offer insights into his trading strategies. Here are key aspects of Ray Dalio's trading philosophy:

1. Principles-Based Approach:

- **Philosophy:** Dalio places a strong emphasis on principles and a systematic approach to decision-making.
- **Strategy:** At Bridgewater, Dalio developed a set of principles that guide the firm's investment strategies. These principles are designed to be consistent and repeatable, providing a framework for decision-making across different market conditions.

2. Economic Cycle Analysis:

- **Philosophy:** Dalio is known for his focus on understanding economic cycles and their impact on financial markets.
- **Strategy:** Bridgewater's investment strategies involve analyzing macroeconomic indicators to determine the stage of the economic cycle. This analysis informs asset allocation decisions and helps identify opportunities and risks.

3. Risk Parity:

- **Philosophy:** Dalio popularized the concept of risk parity, where asset allocations are adjusted based on the risk contribution of each asset class.
- **Strategy:** Bridgewater's risk parity approach aims to balance risk across various asset classes, adjusting allocations based on the volatility and risk characteristics of each component. This strategy seeks to achieve a more consistent risk profile.

4. Diversification:

- **Philosophy:** Dalio advocates for diversification as a means of managing risk.
- **Strategy:** Bridgewater's portfolios are diversified across asset classes, geographies, and investment strategies. Diversification is used to mitigate the impact of adverse market movements in any single area.

5. Algorithmic Trading:

- **Philosophy:** Bridgewater utilizes systematic, algorithmic trading strategies.

- **Strategy:** Dalio's firm employs quantitative models and algorithms to make investment decisions. These algorithms are based on the principles established by Dalio and his team, allowing for systematic execution of their strategies.

6. Balanced Approach:

- **Philosophy:** Dalio believes in a balanced approach to investing, considering both upside potential and downside risk.
- **Strategy:** Bridgewater seeks to balance portfolios to achieve a desirable risk-reward profile. This approach aligns with the firm's risk parity strategy, aiming to generate consistent returns while managing risk effectively.

7. Realistic Assessment of Market Conditions:

- **Philosophy:** Dalio emphasizes the importance of a realistic assessment of market conditions and a willingness to adapt to changing environments.
- **Strategy:** Bridgewater actively monitors economic indicators and adjusts its investment strategies based on the evolving macroeconomic landscape. This adaptability allows the firm to navigate different market environments.

8. Dealing with Uncertainty:

- **Philosophy:** Dalio acknowledges the inherent uncertainty in markets and the need to be adaptable.
- **Strategy:** Bridgewater's strategies incorporate robust risk management and scenario analysis to deal with uncertainty. The firm aims to prepare for a range of possible outcomes rather than relying on a single, static forecast.

9. Stress Testing:

- **Philosophy:** Bridgewater emphasizes stress testing portfolios to evaluate their resilience under adverse conditions.
- **Strategy:** The firm conducts stress tests to assess how portfolios would perform during extreme market events. This allows Bridgewater to identify potential vulnerabilities and make adjustments to improve portfolio resilience.

10. Continuous Learning:

- **Philosophy:** Dalio believes in continuous learning and the importance of reflection on both successes and failures.
- **Strategy:** Bridgewater places a strong emphasis on learning from experiences, conducting post-mortems on trades and strategies to improve decision-making. This commitment to continuous learning contributes to the firm's ability to adapt and evolve.

It's essential to note that Ray Dalio's strategies, as implemented by Bridgewater Associates, are sophisticated and tailored to the firm's institutional approach to managing investments. Individual investors should carefully consider their risk tolerance, investment goals, and time horizons when drawing inspiration from Dalio's principles. Additionally, Bridgewater's success is attributed to a team-based approach and the collaboration of skilled professionals in the firm.

6. Richard Dennis (1949–2018):

Overview: Richard Dennis was a commodities trader and founder of the Turtle Traders. In the 1980s, he conducted an experiment to prove that trading skills could be taught, leading to the success of the Turtle Traders who achieved significant profits.

Key Lessons: The Turtle Traders' success demonstrated the effectiveness of a systematic and disciplined trading approach.

Trading strategies

Richard Dennis, a commodities trader, and founder of the Turtle Traders is known for developing and implementing a successful trend-following trading strategy. Here are key elements of Richard Dennis's trading strategy:

1. Trend Following:

- **Philosophy:** Dennis believed in the effectiveness of trend following strategies, which involve identifying and riding the prevailing market trends.

- **Strategy:** The Turtle Traders, a group of traders trained by Dennis, were taught to identify and follow trends using technical analysis. This involved using indicators to recognize the direction of a trend and initiating trades in the direction of that trend.

2. Donchian Channel Breakout:

- **Philosophy:** Dennis popularized the use of Donchian Channels for breakout trading.

- **Strategy:** The Donchian Channel is an indicator that plots the highest high and lowest low over a specified period. Dennis and the Turtle Traders used breakouts from these channels as signals to enter trades. For example, a long trade might be initiated when the price breaks above the highest high of the specified period.

3. Position Sizing:

- **Philosophy:** Dennis recognized the importance of proper position sizing to manage risk effectively.

- **Strategy:** The Turtle Traders used a systematic approach to position sizing based on the concept of "volatility normalization." This involved adjusting the size of each trade based on the volatility of the market, aiming to standardize risk across different asset classes.

4. Diversification:

- **Philosophy:** Dennis advocated for diversification to spread risk across different markets.
- **Strategy:** The Turtle Traders traded a diversified portfolio of commodities, currencies, and financial futures. Diversification was seen as a way to reduce the impact of adverse movements in any single market.

5. Rigid Discipline:

- **Philosophy:** Dennis emphasized the importance of discipline in following the trading rules consistently.
- **Strategy:** The Turtle Traders were required to adhere strictly to the predefined rules of the trading system. This included entering and exiting trades based on specific criteria without allowing emotions to influence decision-making.

6. Systematic Rules:

- **Philosophy:** Dennis believed in having a systematic and rule-based approach to trading.
- **Strategy:** The Turtle Traders followed a set of mechanical rules for entering and exiting trades. These rules were designed to remove subjectivity and emotions from the trading process.

7. Pyramiding:

- **Philosophy:** Dennis and the Turtle Traders used a pyramiding strategy to add to winning positions.
- **Strategy:** When a trade was profitable, additional positions were added in the direction of the trend. This strategy aimed to maximize profits during strong and sustained market trends.

8. Long-Term Perspective:

- **Philosophy:** Dennis took a longer-term perspective in trading and did not focus on short-term fluctuations.
- **Strategy:** The Turtle Traders typically held positions for a more extended period, allowing trends to play out. This approach required patience and the ability to withstand shorter-term market noise.

9. Risk Management:

- **Philosophy:** Dennis stressed the importance of risk management in trading.

- **Strategy:** The Turtle Traders used systematic risk management techniques, including setting stop-loss orders to limit potential losses. The volatility normalization approach also contributed to managing risk across different markets.

10. Continuous Improvement:

- **Philosophy:** Dennis believed in the need for continuous improvement and adaptation.
- **Strategy:** The trading system used by the Turtle Traders was not static; it underwent refinement and adaptation as market conditions changed. This commitment to continuous improvement was crucial for staying relevant in evolving markets.

Richard Dennis's trading strategies, particularly those taught to the Turtle Traders, exemplify the effectiveness of systematic, trend-following approaches with a strong emphasis on risk management and discipline. While his strategies were successful in their time, it's important for traders to recognize that market conditions can change, and adaptability is key for long-term success.

7. Ed Seykota (b. 1946):

Overview: Ed Seykota is a pioneer in the field of computerized trading systems. He gained recognition for his success in developing and implementing trend-following systems, achieving significant returns.

Key Lessons: Seykota is known for his emphasis on trend following, risk management, and the use of algorithmic trading systems.

Trading strategies

Ed Seykota, a pioneer in the field of computerized trading systems, is known for his success in developing and implementing trend-following strategies. Here are key elements of Ed Seykota's trading strategies:

1. Trend Following:

- **Philosophy:** Seykota is a strong advocate of trend following, believing that markets exhibit trends that can be identified and exploited for profitable trading.
- **Strategy:** Seykota's trading systems are designed to identify and ride trends, whether they are upward (bullish) or downward (bearish). He uses technical analysis and indicators to determine the direction of the prevailing trend.

2. Systematic Trading:

- **Philosophy:** Seykota emphasizes the importance of systematic, rule-based trading approaches.

- **Strategy:** Seykota is known for developing and using computerized trading systems that follow predefined rules. These systems remove emotional biases and subjectivity from trading decisions, providing a disciplined approach.

3. Risk Management:

- **Philosophy:** Seykota places significant importance on risk management to protect capital and preserve long-term profitability.
- **Strategy:** He uses risk management techniques, including setting stop-loss orders, position sizing based on risk tolerance, and overall portfolio risk control. Seykota's focus on managing risk is integral to his trading strategy.

4. Position Sizing:

- **Philosophy:** Seykota understands the impact of position sizing on overall portfolio performance.
- **Strategy:** His position sizing approach involves determining the size of a trade based on the level of risk the trader is willing to take. This ensures that each trade contributes an appropriate amount to the overall risk of the portfolio.

5. Technical Analysis:

- **Philosophy:** Seykota relies on technical analysis for decision-making, utilizing price charts and indicators.
- **Strategy:** His trading systems incorporate technical analysis tools to identify trends, potential entry and exit points, and overall market conditions. Seykota believes that historical price data can provide valuable insights for making informed trading decisions.

6. Mechanical Trading Systems:

- **Philosophy:** Seykota advocates for the use of mechanical trading systems to remove emotional influences from trading.
- **Strategy:** His approach involves developing and employing mechanical trading systems that follow specific rules. These systems are backtested to ensure historical viability and then implemented in live markets.

7. Cutting Losses and Letting Profits Run:

- **Philosophy:** Seykota follows the classic trading adage of cutting losses quickly and letting profits run.
- **Strategy:** When a trade goes against him, Seykota is quick to cut losses by adhering to predetermined stop-loss levels. On the other hand, he allows winning trades to continue as long as the trend remains intact, maximizing profits during favorable market conditions.

8. Adaptability:

- **Philosophy:** Seykota recognizes the need for adaptability in trading as market conditions change.
- **Strategy:** While Seykota's core principles remain consistent, he is open to adapting his trading systems and strategies to evolving market dynamics. This adaptability is crucial for staying relevant and effective over time.

9. Continuous Learning:

- **Philosophy:** Seykota values continuous learning and improvement in trading.
- **Strategy:** He believes that markets evolve, and traders must adapt and learn continuously to stay ahead. Seykota reviews and refines his trading systems based on ongoing analysis and experience.

10. Emotional Discipline:

- **Philosophy:** Seykota emphasizes the need for emotional discipline in trading.
- **Strategy:** By relying on systematic, rule-based approaches and avoiding impulsive decisions, Seykota minimizes the impact of emotions on trading. Emotional discipline is essential for maintaining consistency and following the trading plan.

Ed Seykota's trading strategies, particularly his focus on trend following, systematic trading, risk management, and adaptability, have influenced many traders and investors. While the specifics of his systems may vary, the underlying principles can provide valuable insights for those seeking to develop disciplined and effective trading approaches.

8. Nicolas Darvas (1920–1977):

Overview: Nicolas Darvas was a dancer and self-taught investor who achieved significant success in the stock market. He documented his trading experiences in the book "How I Made $2,000,000 in the Stock Market."

Key Lessons: Darvas focused on technical analysis, trend following, and the use of stop-loss orders to manage risk.

Trading strategies

Nicolas Darvas was a professional dancer and self-taught investor who became famous for his success in the stock market. He documented his trading experiences in the book "How I Made $2,000,000 in the Stock Market." Here are key elements of Nicolas Darvas's trading strategies:

1. Box Theory:

- **Philosophy:** Darvas developed the "Box Theory" to identify and trade stocks with clear trends.

- **Strategy:** He looked for stocks that were trading within a defined price range or "box." When a stock broke out of the box to the upside, Darvas saw it as a bullish signal, and he would enter a long position. Conversely, a break to the downside signaled a bearish move, prompting him to consider short positions.

2. Techno-Fundamental Approach:

- **Philosophy:** Darvas combined technical analysis with some fundamental analysis.
- **Strategy:** While he primarily used technical indicators and chart patterns to identify trading opportunities, Darvas also considered the overall market conditions and the potential for a stock to experience sustained growth based on its fundamentals.

3. Volume Confirmation:

- **Philosophy:** Darvas believed in using volume as a confirmation signal for price movements.
- **Strategy:** When a stock broke out of its box on high volume, Darvas saw it as a confirmation of a strong move. High volume indicated increased market interest and participation, reinforcing the validity of the breakout.

4. Stop-Loss Orders:

- **Philosophy:** Darvas placed great importance on risk management.
- **Strategy:** He used stop-loss orders to manage risk. If a stock moved against him and triggered the stop-loss, he would exit the position to limit potential losses. This disciplined approach helped him control risk and preserve capital.

5. No Prediction of Market Direction:

- **Philosophy:** Darvas did not attempt to predict the overall market direction.
- **Strategy:** Instead of forecasting the market, he focused on individual stocks that showed clear trends. By following the price action of specific stocks, he aimed to capitalize on their inherent movements, regardless of broader market trends.

6. Emphasis on Stock Selection:

- **Philosophy:** Darvas believed in the importance of selecting the right stocks for trading.
- **Strategy:** He sought stocks with strong fundamentals, clear trends, and those exhibiting a series of boxes, indicating a potential for sustained price movements. His emphasis on stock selection was a key factor in his trading success.

7. Continuous Monitoring:

- **Philosophy:** Darvas closely monitored his trades and the market.
- **Strategy:** He dedicated time each day to review his positions and market conditions. His continuous monitoring allowed him to stay informed about the progress of his trades and make timely decisions.

8. Remote Trading:

- **Philosophy:** Darvas preferred a hands-off approach to trading.
- **Strategy:** As a touring dancer, he was often on the move. Darvas relied on his broker to execute trades based on the instructions he sent by telegram. This remote trading approach allowed him to maintain his trading activities while pursuing his dancing career.

9. Learning from Mistakes:

- **Philosophy:** Darvas learned from both successes and failures.
- **Strategy:** He analyzed his trades, identified what worked and what didn't, and adapted his strategies accordingly. This commitment to learning from mistakes contributed to his ongoing success.

10. Patience and Discipline:

- **Philosophy:** Darvas exercised patience and discipline in his trading.
- **Strategy:** He waited for clear signals and confirmation before entering trades. His systematic and disciplined approach, coupled with the ability to wait for the right opportunities, was crucial to his success.

Nicolas Darvas's trading strategies, especially the Box Theory, have inspired traders to focus on identifying trends and using systematic approaches to manage risk. His emphasis on continuous learning and adapting to market conditions remains relevant for traders seeking long-term success.

9. Bernard Baruch (1870–1965):

Overview: Bernard Baruch was a financier, statesman, and presidential adviser. He became one of the best-known speculators in the early 20th century, navigating various market cycles and political changes.

Key Lessons: Baruch's success was attributed to his understanding of market sentiment, economic factors, and a disciplined approach to investing.

Trading strategies

Bernard Baruch, a financier, statesman, and adviser to several U.S. presidents, was known for his success in the stock market. While his trading strategies were not explicitly documented in a systematic way, there are key principles that can be gleaned from his experiences and writings. Here are some aspects of Bernard Baruch's approach to trading:

1. Research and Information:

- **Philosophy:** Baruch emphasized the importance of thorough research and staying informed.
- **Strategy:** He was known for his meticulous research on companies and industries. Baruch believed in staying ahead of market trends by gathering as much information as possible about the companies in which he invested.

2. Economic Analysis:

- **Philosophy:** Baruch considered broader economic trends and conditions.
- **Strategy:** He took into account the overall economic climate and its potential impact on the market. Baruch's ability to assess economic conditions allowed him to position his investments accordingly.

3. Contrarian Approach:

- **Philosophy:** Baruch was known for adopting a contrarian stance.
- **Strategy:** He often went against prevailing market sentiment, buying when others were selling and vice versa. Baruch believed that markets could be irrational, and he sought opportunities when he perceived discrepancies between market prices and intrinsic values.

4. Long-Term Investing:

- **Philosophy:** Baruch had a long-term perspective on investing.
- **Strategy:** While actively trading, Baruch also held onto investments for extended periods, allowing them to appreciate over time. His long-term approach aligned with his confidence in the fundamental strength of the companies he chose.

5. Risk Management:

- **Philosophy:** Baruch was cautious about risk and focused on capital preservation.
- **Strategy:** He implemented risk management measures, including diversification and setting stop-loss orders, to protect his capital. Baruch understood the importance of managing downside risk in order to survive and thrive in the market.

6. Adaptability:

- **Philosophy:** Baruch recognized the need to adapt to changing market conditions.
- **Strategy:** He understood that markets evolve, and successful traders need to be adaptable. Baruch was open to adjusting his strategies in response to shifts in market dynamics or economic circumstances.

7. Timing and Patience:

- **Philosophy:** Baruch valued timing and exercised patience.
- **Strategy:** He believed in waiting for the right opportunities to present themselves. Baruch was patient, not succumbing to impulsive trading decisions, and waited for market conditions that aligned with his analysis.

8. Discipline and Emotional Control:

- **Philosophy:** Baruch stressed the importance of discipline and emotional control.
- **Strategy:** He maintained a disciplined approach to trading, avoiding emotional reactions to short-term market fluctuations. Baruch's ability to keep emotions in check contributed to his success.

9. Political and Geopolitical Analysis:

- **Philosophy:** Baruch considered political and geopolitical factors in his analysis.
- **Strategy:** He recognized that political events and global dynamics could impact the markets. Baruch's ability to integrate political and geopolitical analysis into his decision-making process allowed him to anticipate market movements.

10. Continuous Learning:

- **Philosophy:** Baruch valued continuous learning and adaptation.
- **Strategy:** He believed in staying informed and learning from both successes and failures. Baruch's commitment to ongoing education contributed to his ability to navigate different market environments.

While Bernard Baruch's specific trading strategies may not be extensively documented, his general principles of thorough research, contrarian thinking, long-term perspective, and adaptability remain relevant to traders and investors today. Baruch's multifaceted approach, combining economic analysis, risk management, and a deep understanding of market dynamics, provides timeless lessons for those navigating the complexities of financial markets.

10. William J. O'Neil (1933–2019):

Overview: William J. O'Neil was an American entrepreneur, stockbroker, and founder of Investor's Business Daily. He is known for his proprietary stock research and the development of the CAN SLIM investing strategy.

Key Lessons: O'Neil's approach combines technical analysis, fundamental analysis, and a focus on identifying growth stocks with strong momentum.

Trading strategies

William J. O'Neil was a stockbroker, author, and founder of Investor's Business Daily. He was known for his expertise in stock market analysis and his innovative trading strategies. Here are key elements of William J. O'Neil's trading strategies:

1. CAN SLIM Methodology:

- **Philosophy:** O'Neil developed the CAN SLIM method, a comprehensive approach to selecting stocks with strong growth potential.
- **Strategy:** CAN SLIM stands for:
  - **C - Current Earnings:** Focus on stocks with strong recent earnings growth.
  - **A - Annual Earnings:** Look for companies with consistently high annual earnings.
  - **N - New Products, New Management, New Highs:** Seek companies with new developments and stocks hitting new highs.
  - **S - Supply and Demand:** Analyze the stock's demand and supply dynamics.
  - **L - Leader or Laggard:** Invest in market leaders rather than laggards.
  - **I - Institutional Sponsorship:** Prefer stocks with institutional support.
  - **M - Market Direction:** Trade in the direction of the overall market trend.

2. Technical Analysis:

- **Philosophy:** O'Neil was a proponent of using technical analysis to identify potential trades.
- **Strategy:** He emphasized the importance of analyzing price and volume patterns to identify trends and potential breakouts. O'Neil used charts to identify optimal entry and exit points for trades.

3. Cup and Handle Pattern:

- **Philosophy:** O'Neil popularized the Cup and Handle pattern as a bullish continuation pattern.
- **Strategy:** The Cup and Handle is a technical pattern that indicates a potential upward trend continuation. O'Neil looked for stocks exhibiting this pattern as a signal for potential buying opportunities.

4. Relative Strength:

- **Philosophy:** O'Neil gave importance to relative strength as an indicator of a stock's performance compared to the broader market.
- **Strategy:** Stocks with strong relative strength were favored, as they were perceived to have better resilience during market downturns and greater potential for outperformance.

5. Cutting Losses and Letting Profits Run:

- **Philosophy:** O'Neil emphasized the importance of cutting losses quickly and allowing profits to grow.
- **Strategy:** Setting stop-loss orders to limit potential losses and allowing winning trades to run were key tenets of his risk management strategy.

6. Earnings Reports and Announcements:

- **Philosophy:** O'Neil considered earnings reports and announcements as crucial factors in stock analysis.
- **Strategy:** He paid close attention to a company's earnings reports, especially positive surprises, as they could be catalysts for stock price movements.

7. Market Timing:

- **Philosophy:** O'Neil recognized the significance of market timing.
- **Strategy:** O'Neil advocated adjusting trading activity based on the overall market trend. He would shift exposure to stocks based on the current market conditions, aiming to align with the prevailing trend.

8. Volume Analysis:

- **Philosophy:** O'Neil stressed the importance of volume in confirming price trends.
- **Strategy:** He looked for confirmation of price movements through increasing or decreasing volume. Strong price movements accompanied by high volume were considered more significant and reliable.

9. Investor Psychology:

- **Philosophy:** O'Neil incorporated an understanding of investor psychology into his analysis.

- **Strategy:** He recognized the impact of emotions on market behavior and used technical analysis to gauge the sentiment of market participants.

10. Screening for Winning Stocks:

- **Philosophy:** O'Neil advocated for a systematic approach to screening for winning stocks.
- **Strategy:** Investors were encouraged to use screening criteria based on the CAN SLIM principles to identify stocks with high growth potential.

William J. O'Neil's trading strategies, especially the CAN SLIM method and his emphasis on technical analysis and risk management, have influenced generations of traders. His systematic approach to stock selection and his focus on identifying high-potential growth stocks have left a lasting impact on the field of stock market analysis and trading.

Effective Strategies by Cryptocurrency Professionals

In the dynamic world of cryptocurrency trading, certain individuals have risen to extraordinary heights, demonstrating remarkable prowess and accumulating substantial wealth. Top 13 richest crypto traders, showcasing their net worth and influence in the digital asset space.

1. Changpeng Zhao

@cz_binance Net Worth: $96.5 billion

Changpeng Zhao, widely known as CZ, has been a prominent figure in the cryptocurrency industry, demonstrating a keen understanding of business, finance, and trading strategies. As the founder and CEO of Binance, one of the world's largest cryptocurrency exchanges, CZ's success can be attributed to several key strategies:

1. Visionary Leadership:

Business Strategy: CZ's visionary leadership has been instrumental in shaping Binance into a global powerhouse. By envisioning a comprehensive ecosystem for digital assets, he expanded Binance's offerings beyond trading, including launching Binance Coin (BNB), Binance Launchpad, and Binance Smart Chain.

2. Global Expansion:

Business Strategy: Recognizing the global nature of the cryptocurrency market, CZ strategically expanded Binance's operations worldwide. This global reach has enabled Binance to cater to a diverse user base, fostering mass adoption and solidifying its position as an international leader.

3. Diverse Product Offerings:

Business Strategy: Binance's success stems from its diverse product offerings. In addition to spot trading, Binance introduced futures trading, staking, savings, and a myriad of financial products. This diversification appeals to a broad spectrum of users, contributing to Binance's overall growth.

4. Innovation and Adaptability:

Business Strategy: CZ has shown a commitment to innovation by consistently introducing new features and technologies. Binance Smart Chain, a parallel blockchain to Binance Chain, exemplifies this innovative approach, providing users with a high-performance and low-cost alternative for decentralized applications.

5. Community Engagement:

Business Strategy: CZ actively engages with the cryptocurrency community, fostering a sense of inclusivity. Binance's community-driven approach involves users in decision-making processes, creating a loyal user base and enhancing the platform's overall reputation.

6. Emphasis on Security:

Trading Strategy: Recognizing the importance of security in the crypto space, Binance employs state-of-the-art security measures. This commitment to safeguarding user funds enhances trust and confidence, attracting traders to the platform.

7. Liquidity Management:

Trading Strategy: Binance's strategic focus on maintaining high liquidity contributes to a seamless trading experience. This liquidity attracts institutional traders and enhances the overall efficiency of the platform.

8. User-Centric Approach:

Business Strategy: CZ prioritizes a user-centric approach, continuously refining Binance based on user feedback. This responsiveness to user needs and preferences contributes to the platform's popularity and user satisfaction.

9. Tokenomics:

Finance Strategy: The introduction of Binance Coin (BNB) and its integration into various aspects of the Binance ecosystem demonstrates a sound understanding of tokenomics. BNB's utility, including fee discounts and participation in token sales, adds value to the entire Binance ecosystem.

10. Regulatory Compliance:

Business Strategy: CZ recognizes the importance of regulatory compliance in the evolving crypto landscape. Binance's proactive approach to working with regulators and adapting to changing regulatory environments underscores its commitment to long-term sustainability.

Changpeng Zhao's success in business, finance, and trading reflects a combination of strategic vision, innovation, and a deep understanding of the evolving crypto landscape. As Binance continues to evolve, CZ's strategies contribute to the platform's resilience and ongoing success in the dynamic world of cryptocurrencies.

2. Satoshi

Net Worth: $45.8 billion

Satoshi Nakamoto, the pseudonymous creator of Bitcoin, remains an enigmatic figure, and little is known about their personal identity. Nevertheless, Satoshi's contributions to the world of cryptocurrency and blockchain have left an indelible mark. While the term "trading" may not directly apply to Satoshi, their impact on business and finance, as well as their strategic decisions, can be explored:

1. Invention of Bitcoin:

Innovative Strategy: Satoshi's creation of Bitcoin in 2009 marked the birth of decentralized digital currency. This groundbreaking invention revolutionized the financial landscape by introducing a peer-to-peer electronic cash system, fundamentally changing how people perceive and engage in financial transactions.

2. Decentralization Philosophy:

Business and Finance Strategy: Satoshi's commitment to decentralization is evident in the design of Bitcoin. By eliminating the need for intermediaries like banks, Satoshi aimed to empower individuals with direct control over their finances. This philosophy laid the foundation for a decentralized financial revolution.

3. Anonymity and Privacy:

Business Strategy: Satoshi's decision to remain anonymous reflects a strategic approach to privacy. By stepping away from the public eye, Satoshi allowed the technology to speak for itself, fostering a community-driven development model without a centralized authority figure.

4. Limited Supply of Bitcoin:

Finance Strategy: Satoshi implemented a capped supply of 21 million bitcoins, creating scarcity and deflationary pressure. This deliberate scarcity has contributed to Bitcoin's value proposition as a store of value, akin to precious metals like gold.

5. Open-Source Development:

Business Strategy: Satoshi released the Bitcoin code as open source, inviting collaboration from a global community. This strategy encouraged transparency, peer review, and widespread adoption, fostering a collaborative environment that persists in the broader blockchain space.

6. Mining Incentives:

Finance Strategy: Satoshi introduced the concept of mining rewards to incentivize participants to secure the network. This innovative approach not only ensured the integrity of the blockchain but also created a mechanism for the distribution of new bitcoins, driving interest and participation.

7. Time-Release Distribution:

Finance Strategy: Satoshi's decision to release bitcoins gradually over time, known as the "halving" process, added an element of predictability to the supply. This unique distribution strategy has become a significant event in the cryptocurrency calendar, impacting market dynamics.

8. Community Engagement:

Business Strategy: Although Satoshi eventually stepped back from active development, their engagement with the early Bitcoin community demonstrated a commitment to fostering collaboration and sharing ideas. This community-driven ethos laid the groundwork for the broader cryptocurrency movement.

9. Whitepaper as a Blueprint:

Business and Finance Strategy: Satoshi's publication of the Bitcoin whitepaper served as a strategic blueprint for the development and adoption of the cryptocurrency. This clear and concise document outlined the principles, mechanics, and vision behind Bitcoin, serving as a guiding document for its evolution.

10. Trustless and Permissionless System:

Business and Finance Strategy: Satoshi's creation of a trustless and permissionless system, where users don't need intermediaries to transact, aligns with a strategic vision of financial inclusion and empowerment. This approach challenges traditional financial models and empowers individuals globally.

While Satoshi Nakamoto's strategies may not align with traditional business, finance, and trading practices, their innovative decisions and the creation of Bitcoin have had profound implications on these domains. Satoshi's legacy lies not only in the technological advancements but also in reshaping fundamental concepts of trust, decentralization, and financial sovereignty.

3. Brian Armstrong

@brian_armstrong Net Worth: $10.4 billion

Brian Armstrong, the co-founder and CEO of Coinbase, has played a pivotal role in the growth and mainstream adoption of cryptocurrencies. His strategic decisions and leadership have positioned Coinbase as a leading cryptocurrency exchange. Here are key aspects of Brian Armstrong's successful business, finance, and trading strategies:

1. User-Friendly Platform:

Business Strategy: Under Armstrong's leadership, Coinbase has prioritized creating a user-friendly platform. The simplicity of the interface has contributed to mass adoption by making it easy for beginners to buy, sell, and store cryptocurrencies.

2. Early Embrace of Regulatory Compliance:

Business Strategy: Recognizing the importance of regulatory compliance, Armstrong took early steps to work with regulators. This proactive approach has helped Coinbase establish a reputation for compliance and gain the trust of institutional investors and users.

3. Diverse Cryptocurrency Offerings:

Business Strategy: Coinbase, under Armstrong's guidance, has expanded its cryptocurrency offerings beyond Bitcoin. The platform's support for a diverse range of cryptocurrencies has attracted a broad user base and positioned Coinbase as a comprehensive cryptocurrency exchange.

4. Institutional Focus:

Business Strategy: Armstrong strategically shifted Coinbase's focus to cater to institutional investors. This move has facilitated the influx of institutional funds into the cryptocurrency market, contributing to the maturation and credibility of the industry.

5. Coinbase Pro:

Trading Strategy: Coinbase Pro, the advanced trading platform by Coinbase, caters to professional and experienced traders. This strategic expansion allows Coinbase to serve both novice and seasoned traders, broadening its market reach.

6. Educational Initiatives:

Business Strategy: Armstrong has emphasized education in the cryptocurrency space. Coinbase's educational resources, such as Coinbase Learn, aim to empower users with knowledge about various cryptocurrencies and blockchain technology.

7. Global Expansion:

Business Strategy: Coinbase's strategic approach to global expansion has allowed it to serve users in various countries. This international presence not only broadens Coinbase's user base but also positions it as a global player in the cryptocurrency industry.

8. Custodial Services:

Business and Finance Strategy: Recognizing the need for secure storage solutions, Armstrong expanded Coinbase's services to include custodial solutions. This strategic move attracts institutional clients seeking a secure and compliant way to store digital assets.

9. Listing of Prominent Tokens:

Finance Strategy: Coinbase's strategic decision to list prominent tokens has had a significant impact on the market. The listing of tokens like Ethereum (ETH) and others has provided users with access to a wide array of digital assets.

10. Direct Listing on Nasdaq:

Business Strategy: In a landmark move, Coinbase went public through a direct listing on Nasdaq. This strategic decision not only brought mainstream attention to the cryptocurrency industry but also positioned Coinbase as a publicly traded company.

11. NFT Marketplace:

Business Strategy: Coinbase's entry into the NFT (Non-Fungible Token) space aligns with the growing trend of digital ownership. The NFT marketplace on Coinbase strategically taps into the rising popularity of digital collectibles.

12. Staking Services:

Finance Strategy: Coinbase's introduction of staking services allows users to earn rewards on their cryptocurrencies. This strategic move provides an additional income stream for users while contributing to the overall growth of the platform.

Brian Armstrong's strategic decisions have not only propelled Coinbase to the forefront of the cryptocurrency industry but have also played a role in shaping the broader financial landscape. His focus on accessibility, compliance, and innovation has contributed to Coinbase's success as a user-friendly and trusted platform in the evolving world of digital assets.

4. Chris Larsen

@chrislarsensf Net Worth: $6 billion

Chris Larsen, co-founder of Ripple, has been a key figure in the cryptocurrency space, focusing on solutions for cross-border payments. His strategic decisions have shaped the development and adoption of Ripple's technology. Here are the key elements of Chris Larsen's successful business, finance, and trading strategies:

1. Founding Ripple and XRP:

Business Strategy: Larsen's vision for Ripple was to create a blockchain-based platform that facilitates faster and more cost-effective cross-border payments. The introduction of XRP, Ripple's native cryptocurrency, served as a key component in achieving this vision.

2. Focus on Cross-Border Payments:

Business Strategy: Recognizing the inefficiencies in traditional cross-border payment systems, Larsen strategically positioned Ripple as a solution for financial institutions seeking faster and more cost-effective international transactions.

3. Partnerships with Financial Institutions:

Business Strategy: Larsen led Ripple to establish partnerships with numerous financial institutions globally. These partnerships aimed to integrate Ripple's technology into traditional banking systems, facilitating the seamless transfer of funds across borders.

4. Development of RippleNet:

Business and Finance Strategy: Larsen played a pivotal role in the development of RippleNet, Ripple's decentralized network that connects banks and financial institutions. RippleNet enables real-time, cross-border payments, contributing to increased efficiency in the global financial system.

5. Introduction of Ripple's Suite of Products:

Business Strategy: Under Larsen's leadership, Ripple introduced a suite of products, including xCurrent, xRapid (now known as On-Demand Liquidity), and xVia. Each product addresses specific challenges in the cross-border payments space, providing a comprehensive solution for financial institutions.

6. XRP as a Bridge Currency:

Finance Strategy: Larsen advocated for XRP as a bridge currency in cross-border transactions. The use of XRP as a bridge asset aims to minimize liquidity costs and increase the speed of transactions between different fiat currencies.

7. Regulatory Engagement:

Business Strategy: Larsen has been actively engaged in discussions with regulators to ensure compliance with financial regulations. This strategic approach aims to build trust among financial institutions and regulatory bodies, fostering a conducive environment for Ripple's adoption.

8. Global Expansion:

Business Strategy: Larsen's strategic focus on global expansion has led Ripple to establish a presence in various regions. This global approach enhances Ripple's ability to cater to a diverse set of financial institutions and meet the unique challenges of different markets.

9. Interoperability Initiatives:

Business Strategy: Larsen has shown a commitment to interoperability by participating in initiatives that connect different blockchain networks. This strategic approach aligns with the broader goal of creating a seamless and interconnected global financial ecosystem.

10. Commitment to Financial Inclusion:

Business Strategy: Larsen's vision extends beyond established financial institutions to include the unbanked and underbanked populations. Ripple's technology aims to facilitate financial inclusion by providing accessible and efficient payment solutions.

11. Focus on Environmental Sustainability:

Business Strategy: More recently, Larsen has expressed a commitment to environmental sustainability in blockchain technology. This strategic focus aligns with growing concerns about the environmental impact of certain blockchain networks.

Chris Larsen's strategies have positioned Ripple as a significant player in the fintech and blockchain space. His emphasis on solving real-world problems in cross-border payments and engagement with regulatory bodies reflects a strategic vision for Ripple's role in shaping the future of global finance.

5. Tyler Winklevoss

@tyler and Cameron Winklevoss

@cameron Net Worth: $5.3 billion each

The Winklevoss twins, early Bitcoin investors and founders of the Gemini cryptocurrency exchange, have been influential figures in shaping the regulatory environment for digital assets. Their commitment to fostering a secure and regulated crypto ecosystem has been commendable.

1. Founding Gemini:

Business Strategy: Tyler Winklevoss, alongside Cameron, co-founded Gemini with a vision to create a secure and regulated platform for buying, selling, and storing cryptocurrencies. The emphasis on regulatory compliance aimed to build trust among users and regulators.

2. Regulatory Compliance:

Business Strategy: Gemini has positioned itself as a fully regulated cryptocurrency exchange. Tyler's commitment to regulatory compliance reflects a strategic approach to navigate the evolving regulatory landscape, providing users with a secure and compliant trading environment.

3. Trust and Security:

Business Strategy: Tyler recognizes the importance of trust and security in the cryptocurrency space. Gemini's focus on robust security measures, including insurance coverage for digital assets, aligns with a strategic commitment to building a trustworthy platform.

4. Institutional Focus:

Business Strategy: Gemini has strategically positioned itself to serve institutional clients. This focus on institutional investors contributes to market liquidity, attracts larger trades, and enhances Gemini's standing as a platform suitable for a broad range of users.

5. Cryptocurrency Education:

Business Strategy: Tyler Winklevoss has actively engaged in cryptocurrency education initiatives. Gemini's commitment to educating users through blog posts, newsletters, and educational content aligns with a strategic goal of fostering a knowledgeable user base.

6. The Winklevoss Twins' Advocacy for Bitcoin:

Business and Finance Strategy: Both Tyler and Cameron have been vocal advocates for Bitcoin. Their strategic approach involves promoting the narrative of Bitcoin as digital gold and a store of value, contributing to the broader adoption and acceptance of Bitcoin in the financial landscape.

7. Introduction of the Gemini Dollar (GUSD):

Finance Strategy: Gemini introduced the Gemini Dollar (GUSD), a stablecoin pegged to the U.S. dollar. This strategic move addresses the need for a stable and reliable digital representation of traditional fiat currency within the Gemini ecosystem.

8. Gemini Exchange-Traded Funds (ETF) Proposals:

Finance Strategy: The Winklevoss twins have consistently pursued the approval of a Bitcoin ETF. The strategic intent is to provide traditional investors with a regulated and accessible way to gain exposure to Bitcoin, potentially opening the doors to a broader investor base.

9. NFT Marketplace:

Business Strategy: Gemini's entry into the NFT space, offering a marketplace for digital collectibles, aligns with the growing trend of non-fungible tokens. This strategic move taps into the increasing interest in digital ownership and unique digital assets.

10. Commitment to Self-Regulation:

Business Strategy: Tyler Winklevoss has advocated for the cryptocurrency industry to embrace self-regulation. This strategic stance aims to proactively address concerns around market integrity and consumer protection, fostering a responsible and sustainable industry.

11. Digital Asset Custody Services:

Business Strategy: Recognizing the importance of secure storage for digital assets, Gemini offers custody services. This strategic move caters to institutional clients and individuals seeking a reliable and secure solution for storing their cryptocurrencies.

Tyler Winklevoss's strategies for Gemini reflect a commitment to regulatory compliance, security, and the long-term growth of the cryptocurrency ecosystem. His focus on education and the institutionalization of the cryptocurrency market positions Gemini as a trusted and evolving platform in the rapidly changing world of digital assets.

6. Mike Novogratz

@novogratz Net Worth: $5 billion

Mike Novogratz, a former hedge fund manager and founder of Galaxy Digital, has been a significant player in the cryptocurrency space. His business, finance, and trading strategies have contributed to the growth of Galaxy Digital and his influence on the broader crypto industry. Here are key elements of Mike Novogratz's successful strategies:

1. Founding Galaxy Digital:

Business Strategy: Novogratz founded Galaxy Digital as a full-service cryptocurrency merchant bank. This strategic move positioned Galaxy Digital to offer a range of services, including trading, asset management, and investment banking within the cryptocurrency and blockchain ecosystem.

2. Advocacy for Institutional Investment:

Business Strategy: Novogratz has been a vocal advocate for institutional involvement in the cryptocurrency market. His strategic focus on institutional investment aims to bring mainstream legitimacy to the industry and increase capital inflows.

3. Investment in Bitcoin and Ethereum:

Finance Strategy: Novogratz strategically invested in Bitcoin and Ethereum, two of the largest cryptocurrencies by market capitalization. This move reflects his belief in the long-term value and potential of these foundational assets within the crypto space.

4. Creation of Galaxy Digital's Trading Arm:

Business Strategy: Galaxy Digital's trading arm actively engages in cryptocurrency trading. This strategic initiative allows the firm to capitalize on market opportunities, provide liquidity, and contribute to the overall trading ecosystem.

5. Cryptocurrency Investment Fund:

Finance Strategy: Novogratz launched a cryptocurrency investment fund under Galaxy Digital, allowing investors exposure to a diversified portfolio of digital assets. This strategic move provides a structured vehicle for investors to participate in the crypto market.

6. Venture Capital Investments:

Business and Finance Strategy: Galaxy Digital engages in venture capital investments in blockchain and cryptocurrency projects. Novogratz's strategic approach involves identifying promising projects and contributing to their development through strategic investments.

7. Focus on Blockchain Technology:

Business Strategy: Novogratz recognizes the transformative potential of blockchain technology beyond cryptocurrencies. Galaxy Digital's strategic focus on blockchain investments aims to tap into the broader applications of decentralized technology across various industries.

8. Bitcoin Price Predictions:

Trading Strategy: Novogratz has made various predictions about Bitcoin's price movements. While cryptocurrency markets are inherently volatile, these predictions, based on market analysis and trends, showcase a strategic approach to understanding and navigating market dynamics.

9. Engagement in Cryptocurrency Advocacy:

Business Strategy: Novogratz actively engages in public discourse and media appearances to advocate for the adoption and acceptance of cryptocurrencies. This strategic communication aims to shape a positive narrative around the industry.

10. Involvement in Cryptocurrency Initiatives:

Business Strategy: Novogratz is involved in various cryptocurrency initiatives, including efforts to promote regulatory clarity and industry standards. His strategic engagement in shaping the regulatory landscape reflects a commitment to a sustainable and compliant crypto ecosystem.

11. Bitcoin Mining Operations:

Business Strategy: Galaxy Digital has engaged in Bitcoin mining operations. Novogratz's strategic decision to enter the mining sector aligns with the broader industry trend and provides additional exposure to Bitcoin's ecosystem.

Mike Novogratz's strategies encompass a broad spectrum, from investments and trading to advocating for industry growth. His business acumen and strategic initiatives have contributed to Galaxy Digital's standing as a key player in the evolving landscape of cryptocurrencies and blockchain technology.

7. Joseph Lubin

@ethereumJoseph Net Worth: $5 billion

Joseph Lubin, a co-founder of Ethereum and founder of ConsenSys, has played a significant role in the development and promotion of blockchain technology. His contributions to the Ethereum ecosystem and strategic initiatives have shaped the decentralized landscape. Here are key elements of Joseph Lubin's successful business, finance, and trading strategies:

1. Co-Founding Ethereum:

Business Strategy: Lubin was one of the co-founders of Ethereum, a blockchain platform that introduced smart contracts. Ethereum's creation addressed limitations in Bitcoin and laid the foundation for a wide range of decentralized applications (DApps).

2. Founding ConsenSys:

Business Strategy: Lubin founded ConsenSys as a blockchain software technology company. This strategic move aimed to provide Ethereum-based solutions, foster developer communities, and contribute to the growth of the Ethereum ecosystem.

3. Building Ethereum Developer Community:

Business Strategy: ConsenSys actively focuses on building and supporting the Ethereum developer community. This strategic initiative aims to ensure a vibrant ecosystem of developers creating applications and solutions on the Ethereum blockchain.

4. Venture Studio Model:

Business Strategy: ConsenSys operates on a venture studio model, incubating and supporting various Ethereum-based projects. This strategic approach allows ConsenSys to diversify its portfolio and contribute to the development of innovative decentralized applications.

5. Enterprise Ethereum Alliance (EEA) Involvement:

Business Strategy: Lubin played a key role in establishing the Enterprise Ethereum Alliance (EEA), a collaboration between enterprises and Ethereum experts. This strategic move aimed to promote the adoption of Ethereum in enterprise environments and foster industry standards.

6. Promoting Tokenization and Decentralized Finance (DeFi):

Business Strategy: Lubin and ConsenSys actively promote the tokenization of assets and the growth of decentralized finance (DeFi) on the Ethereum blockchain. This strategic focus aligns with the broader trend of financial innovation within the blockchain space.

7. Investments in Ethereum-Based Projects:

Finance Strategy: ConsenSys has made strategic investments in various Ethereum-based projects. This approach not only supports the development of promising projects but also aligns with ConsenSys's goal of contributing to a thriving Ethereum ecosystem.

8. Partnerships with Major Companies:

Business Strategy: ConsenSys has formed strategic partnerships with major companies to integrate blockchain solutions. These collaborations aim to explore the potential applications of blockchain technology in various industries, including finance, supply chain, and more.

9. Promoting Ethereum 2.0 Transition:

Business Strategy: Lubin has been actively involved in promoting the transition to Ethereum 2.0, an upgrade aimed at improving scalability and sustainability. This strategic focus reflects a commitment to addressing the challenges of the current Ethereum infrastructure.

10. Educational Initiatives:

Business Strategy: ConsenSys engages in educational initiatives to raise awareness about blockchain and Ethereum. This strategic move aims to foster understanding and adoption by providing resources and training for developers, enterprises, and the wider community.

11. Decentralized Identity Solutions:

Business Strategy: Lubin and ConsenSys have explored decentralized identity solutions on the Ethereum blockchain. This strategic initiative aligns with the broader goal of enhancing privacy and security in online interactions.

12. Involvement in Social Impact Projects:

Business Strategy: ConsenSys has participated in social impact projects using blockchain technology. This strategic engagement demonstrates a commitment to leveraging blockchain for positive social change.

Joseph Lubin's strategies center around the growth and development of the Ethereum ecosystem, with a focus on fostering innovation, supporting developers, and promoting the adoption of decentralized solutions across various industries. His vision extends beyond finance, encompassing the transformative potential of blockchain technology in diverse sectors.

8. Micree Zhan

@MicreeZ Net Worth: $3.2 billion

Micree Zhan, co-founder of Bitmain, has been a prominent figure in the cryptocurrency mining industry. His role in establishing one of the world's leading mining hardware manufacturers, Bitmain, reflects strategic decisions that have shaped the mining landscape. Here are key elements of Micree Zhan's successful business, finance, and trading strategies:

1. Co-Founding Bitmain:

Business Strategy: Zhan played a pivotal role in co-founding Bitmain, a company focused on designing and manufacturing cryptocurrency mining hardware, including ASIC (Application-Specific Integrated Circuit) miners. This strategic move positioned Bitmain as a key player in the mining hardware industry.

2. Dominance in ASIC Mining:

Business Strategy: Bitmain, under Zhan's leadership, became synonymous with ASIC mining dominance. The strategic focus on developing efficient and powerful ASIC miners allowed Bitmain to capture a significant share of the market, enabling miners to efficiently mine cryptocurrencies like Bitcoin.

3. Antminer Series:

Business Strategy: Bitmain's Antminer series, developed under Zhan's guidance, became widely popular among cryptocurrency miners. This strategic product line offered miners powerful and energy-efficient hardware solutions, contributing to Bitmain's success in the competitive mining hardware market.

4. Expanding Product Offerings:

Business Strategy: Zhan led Bitmain to expand its product offerings beyond mining hardware. The company ventured into developing products such as mining pools and other blockchain-related technologies, showcasing a strategic approach to diversifying its portfolio.

5. Global Market Expansion:

Business Strategy: Zhan strategically expanded Bitmain's presence in the global market. This expansion involved establishing partnerships, distribution channels, and service centers worldwide, enabling Bitmain to cater to the growing demand for mining hardware on a global scale.

6. Strategic Partnerships:

Business Strategy: Bitmain, under Zhan's leadership, entered into strategic partnerships with various industry players. These partnerships included collaborations with mining farms, exchanges, and other blockchain companies, contributing to Bitmain's influence in the cryptocurrency ecosystem.

7. Innovation in Cooling Solutions:

Business Strategy: Zhan and Bitmain focused on innovative cooling solutions for mining hardware. The development of effective cooling systems addressed one of the challenges in cryptocurrency mining, enhancing the efficiency and longevity of Bitmain's mining hardware.

8. Bitcoin Cash (BCH) Mining Support:

Finance Strategy: Bitmain, led by Zhan, has been supportive of Bitcoin Cash (BCH) mining. This strategic decision aligned with the company's interests and contributed to the mining ecosystem supporting alternative cryptocurrencies.

9. Navigating Cryptocurrency Market Trends:

Business Strategy: Zhan navigated Bitmain through various trends in the cryptocurrency market. This included adapting to changes in mining algorithms, addressing shifts in market demand, and strategically responding to technological advancements in the blockchain space.

10. Blockchain and AI Exploration:

Business Strategy: Zhan expressed interest in exploring the intersections of blockchain and artificial intelligence (AI). This strategic vision indicates a forward-looking approach to potential synergies between these emerging technologies.

11. Focusing on Energy Efficiency:

Business Strategy: Bitmain, guided by Zhan, has emphasized energy efficiency in mining operations. This strategic focus aligns with broader industry trends toward sustainable and environmentally friendly mining practices.

12. Navigating Regulatory Challenges:

Business Strategy: Zhan has navigated Bitmain through regulatory challenges in various jurisdictions. This strategic approach involves adapting to evolving regulatory landscapes while maintaining Bitmain's position as a leading player in the mining industry.

Micree Zhan's strategies in the cryptocurrency mining industry revolve around innovation in hardware, global market expansion, and strategic partnerships. His leadership at Bitmain has contributed to the company's prominent position in the competitive and rapidly evolving field of cryptocurrency mining.

9. Vitalik Buterin

@VitalikButerin Net Worth: More than $1 billion

Vitalik Buterin, the co-founder of Ethereum, has been a driving force behind the development and advancement of blockchain technology. While Vitalik is known more for his contributions to the technical and philosophical aspects of blockchain, his role in shaping the business and financial landscape cannot be overlooked. Here are key elements of Vitalik Buterin's influence in business, finance, and trading strategies:

1. Co-Founding Ethereum:

Business Strategy: Vitalik played a crucial role in co-founding Ethereum, a blockchain platform designed to support smart contracts and decentralized applications (DApps). This strategic move aimed to provide a versatile and programmable blockchain, fostering innovation and a wide range of use cases.

2. Ethereum as a Development Platform:

Business Strategy: Ethereum, under Vitalik's vision, positioned itself as a development platform for decentralized applications. This strategic focus attracted developers and businesses to build on the Ethereum blockchain, contributing to its ecosystem's growth.

3. ICO Boom and ERC-20 Standard:

Finance Strategy: The introduction of the ERC-20 standard on Ethereum facilitated the Initial Coin Offering (ICO) boom. This strategic move provided a fundraising mechanism for blockchain projects, driving significant capital into the Ethereum ecosystem.

4. Decentralized Finance (DeFi) Advocacy:

Business Strategy: Vitalik has been an advocate for decentralized finance (DeFi) applications on Ethereum. This strategic focus aims to create an open and permissionless financial system, enabling various financial services without traditional intermediaries.

5. Introduction of Ethereum 2.0:

Business Strategy: Vitalik has been actively involved in the development and promotion of Ethereum 2.0. This strategic upgrade addresses scalability and sustainability issues, ensuring Ethereum's continued relevance in the rapidly evolving blockchain landscape.

6. Interoperability Initiatives:

Business Strategy: Vitalik has expressed interest in promoting interoperability between different blockchain networks. This strategic vision aligns with the broader goal of creating a more interconnected and collaborative blockchain ecosystem.

7. Partnerships and Collaboration:

Business Strategy: Vitalik has been involved in forming partnerships and collaborations with various organizations and projects. These strategic alliances contribute to the integration and adoption of Ethereum in diverse industries.

8. Engagement with Developers and Community:

Business Strategy: Vitalik's active engagement with the Ethereum developer community and broader blockchain community is a strategic move. It fosters collaboration, innovation, and a sense of shared ownership in the Ethereum ecosystem.

9. Addressing Scalability Challenges:

Business Strategy: Vitalik has been at the forefront of addressing scalability challenges in Ethereum. Ethereum 2.0, with its move to a proof-of-stake consensus mechanism, is a strategic response to improve scalability and energy efficiency.

10. Philanthropy and Social Impact:

Business Strategy: Vitalik has engaged in philanthropic efforts, including large donations for social impact projects. This strategic involvement aligns with the belief in using blockchain technology for positive social change.

11. Focus on Sustainability:

Business Strategy: Vitalik has advocated for sustainability in blockchain networks. This strategic focus addresses concerns about the environmental impact of blockchain technology, ensuring its long-term viability.

12. Education and Thought Leadership:

Business Strategy: Vitalik's thought leadership and educational initiatives contribute to shaping the narrative around blockchain technology. This strategic approach fosters a deeper understanding of the technology and its potential applications.

While Vitalik Buterin's contributions are more aligned with technology and philosophy, his strategic decisions have significantly influenced the business, finance, and trading strategies within the Ethereum ecosystem and the broader blockchain industry.

10. Matthew Roszak

@matthewroszak Net Worth: More than $1 billion

Matthew Roszak, a prominent figure in the blockchain and cryptocurrency space, has been involved in various successful ventures and initiatives. His contributions to the industry reflect strategic decisions across business, finance, and trading. Here are key elements of Matthew Roszak's successful strategies:

1. Co-Founding Bloq:

Business Strategy: Roszak co-founded Bloq, a blockchain technology company that provides enterprise-grade blockchain solutions. This strategic move positioned Bloq as a player in delivering innovative blockchain solutions for businesses.

2. Blockchain Investments:

Finance Strategy: Roszak has been actively involved in making strategic investments in blockchain and cryptocurrency projects. This approach allows him to support and participate in the growth of promising ventures within the blockchain ecosystem.

3. Tokenization and Digital Assets:

Business Strategy: Roszak has shown interest in tokenization and digital assets. This strategic focus aligns with the broader trend of transforming traditional assets into digital forms, providing new opportunities for liquidity and financial innovation.

4. Blockchain Education:

Business Strategy: Roszak has been engaged in educating and promoting awareness about blockchain technology. This strategic initiative contributes to a better understanding of blockchain's potential and fosters adoption across different industries.

5. Founding Tally Capital:

Business Strategy: Roszak is the founder of Tally Capital, a venture capital firm focused on investments in blockchain and digital currency-related projects. This strategic move positions Tally Capital as a key player in funding innovative initiatives within the blockchain space.

6. Global Blockchain Council:

Business Strategy: Roszak's involvement in the Global Blockchain Council, as a member, showcases a strategic commitment to fostering collaboration and setting industry standards. This involvement contributes to shaping the global landscape of blockchain technology.

7. Blockchain Policy Advocacy:

Business Strategy: Roszak has been involved in advocating for blockchain-friendly policies. This strategic engagement aims to create a conducive regulatory environment for the growth and adoption of blockchain technology.

8. Blockchain Infrastructure Projects:

Business Strategy: Roszak has expressed interest in supporting blockchain infrastructure projects. This strategic focus involves contributing to the development of foundational technologies that enhance the overall functionality and scalability of blockchain networks.

9. Advisory Roles:

Business Strategy: Roszak has served in advisory roles for various blockchain projects and organizations. This strategic involvement allows him to provide guidance and expertise, contributing to the success of these initiatives.

10. Partnerships and Collaborations:

Business Strategy: Roszak has been involved in forming partnerships and collaborations with industry players. These strategic alliances contribute to the integration and interoperability of blockchain solutions, fostering a more connected ecosystem.

11. Interest in Decentralized Finance (DeFi):

Business Strategy: Roszak's interest in decentralized finance (DeFi) aligns with the growing trend of blockchain-based financial services. This strategic focus involves exploring and supporting projects that bring financial services to a decentralized framework.

12. Engagement in Industry Events:

Business Strategy: Roszak's active participation in industry events, conferences, and forums is a strategic move to stay connected with the latest developments, foster networking opportunities, and contribute to thought leadership within the blockchain community.

Matthew Roszak's strategies reflect a multifaceted approach, encompassing investments, education, policy advocacy, and contributions to the technological infrastructure of blockchain. His influence extends across various sectors within the blockchain and cryptocurrency industry.

11. Fred Ehrsam

@FEhrsam Net Worth: More than $1.1 billion

Fred Ehrsam, co-founder of Coinbase and a key figure in the cryptocurrency space, has been influential in shaping the industry. His involvement in founding one of the leading cryptocurrency exchanges and subsequent ventures reflects successful strategies across business, finance, and the broader blockchain ecosystem. Here are key elements of Fred Ehrsam's successful strategies:

1. Co-Founding Coinbase:

Business Strategy: Ehrsam co-founded Coinbase, a user-friendly cryptocurrency exchange. This strategic move aimed to simplify the process of buying, selling, and storing cryptocurrencies, making it accessible to a broader audience.

2. Driving Mainstream Adoption:

Business Strategy: Coinbase, under Ehrsam's leadership, played a pivotal role in driving mainstream adoption of cryptocurrencies. The user-friendly interface and emphasis on compliance contributed to making Coinbase a popular choice for individuals entering the crypto space.

3. Expansion of Cryptocurrency Offerings:

Business Strategy: Ehrsam strategically expanded Coinbase's offerings beyond Bitcoin to include a variety of cryptocurrencies. This move allowed users to access a diverse range of digital assets, contributing to Coinbase's position as a comprehensive cryptocurrency platform.

4. Innovative Trading Features:

Trading Strategy: Coinbase introduced innovative trading features, including easy-to-use interfaces for both beginners and experienced traders. This strategic focus on user experience and functionality contributed to the platform's success in attracting and retaining users.

5. Partnerships and Collaborations:

Business Strategy: Ehrsam has been involved in forming strategic partnerships and collaborations for Coinbase. These partnerships with financial institutions, regulators, and other industry players aimed to establish Coinbase as a trusted and compliant platform.

6. Institutional Focus:

Business Strategy: Coinbase, under Ehrsam's guidance, strategically shifted focus to serve institutional clients. This move contributed to increasing liquidity on the platform and attracting larger trades from institutional investors.

7. Cryptocurrency Education:

Business Strategy: Coinbase actively engaged in cryptocurrency education initiatives. This strategic move aimed to empower users with knowledge about blockchain technology and digital assets, fostering a more informed user base.

8. Venture Capital Investments:

Finance Strategy: Ehrsam, post-Coinbase, has been involved in venture capital investments. This strategic approach allows him to support and contribute to the growth of innovative projects within the broader blockchain and cryptocurrency ecosystem.

9. Blockchain Advocacy:

Business Strategy: Ehrsam has been an advocate for blockchain technology and its potential applications beyond cryptocurrencies. This strategic focus involves exploring the transformative capabilities of blockchain in various industries.

10. NFT and Digital Ownership:

Business Strategy: Ehrsam has shown interest in the realm of non-fungible tokens (NFTs) and digital ownership. This strategic focus aligns with the growing trend of unique digital assets and the exploration of blockchain's role in digital ownership.

11. Thought Leadership:

Business Strategy: Ehrsam's thought leadership, including writings and public speaking, contributes to shaping the narrative around blockchain and cryptocurrency. This strategic approach fosters a deeper understanding and acceptance of the technology.

12. Focus on Decentralization:

Business Strategy: Ehrsam has expressed a focus on the principles of decentralization. This strategic vision involves exploring ways to leverage blockchain technology to create more decentralized and open systems.

Fred Ehrsam's strategies have played a crucial role in the growth of Coinbase and his subsequent ventures. His emphasis on accessibility, education, and partnerships has contributed to the broader adoption of cryptocurrencies and blockchain technology.

12. Nikil Viswanathan

@nikil Net Worth: More than $1.8 billion

Nikil Viswanathan, co-founder of Alchemy, has been at the forefront of blockchain infrastructure development. His work has facilitated the creation and scaling of decentralized applications.

1. Co-Founding Alchemy:

Business Strategy: Nikil's co-founding of Alchemy indicates a strategic move to provide blockchain infrastructure solutions. This could involve enabling developers to build and scale decentralized applications (DApps), showcasing a commitment to the foundational aspects of the blockchain ecosystem.

2. Blockchain Infrastructure Services:

Business Strategy: Alchemy, under Nikil's leadership, likely focuses on offering essential infrastructure services for blockchain development. This strategic move contributes to the overall growth and efficiency of decentralized applications.

3. Developer-Centric Approach:

Business Strategy: If Alchemy adopts a developer-centric approach, it would reflect a strategic emphasis on empowering developers to easily work with blockchain technology. Such an approach could attract a broader audience of developers to leverage Alchemy's infrastructure.

4. API Platform for Blockchain:

Business Strategy: Alchemy may operate as an API platform for blockchain, providing a set of tools and services for developers to interact with blockchain networks. This strategic positioning can simplify development processes and foster innovation in the blockchain space.

5. Scalability Solutions:

Business Strategy: If Alchemy addresses scalability challenges in blockchain development, it would reflect a strategic focus on improving the efficiency and performance of decentralized applications. This can be crucial for the widespread adoption of blockchain technology.

6. Funding and Investments:

Finance Strategy: Alchemy's funding and investment activities, if any, could indicate strategic financial decisions aimed at supporting the company's growth and expansion. This may involve securing funding from venture capital firms or engaging in strategic partnerships.

7. Strategic Partnerships:

Business Strategy: Nikil's involvement in forming strategic partnerships for Alchemy could signify a commitment to collaboration and integration within the blockchain ecosystem. Such partnerships can enhance the platform's utility and reach.

8. Adoption and Integration:

Business Strategy: If Alchemy actively seeks adoption by major blockchain projects and integrates its services into various decentralized applications, it would reflect a strategic effort to become a widely-used infrastructure provider.

9. Blockchain Education and Advocacy:

Business Strategy: A focus on blockchain education and advocacy efforts by Nikil and Alchemy could be a strategic move to contribute to the understanding and acceptance of blockchain technology, fostering a supportive ecosystem.

10. Market Positioning:

Business Strategy: Alchemy's market positioning, including its target audience and competitive differentiators, would be part of its strategic plan. This involves identifying market needs and positioning the platform effectively within the blockchain industry.

Please note that the specifics of Nikil Viswanathan's strategies for Alchemy may be subject to change, and for the latest and most accurate information, it's recommended to refer to official announcements from Alchemy or Nikil Viswanathan directly.

ABOUT THE AUTHOR

As you immerse yourself in the insights of "Trade Phenomena," consider Rana as your guide, offering a roadmap to financial success and self-reliance in the dynamic world of trading.

www.ingramcontent.com/pod-product-compliance
Lightning Source LLC
Chambersburg PA
CBHW072300260726
48658CB00004BA/1326